GLOBALISATION AND RURAL DEVELOPMENT

GLOBALISATION AND RURAL DEVELOPMENT

S. Dharmaraj

ABHIJEET PUBLICATIONS
DELHI 110 094

ABHIJEET PUBLICATIONS
2/46 Tukhmeerpur Extension
Delhi-110 094
Phone: 011-22960492, 65698474
E-mail: abhijeetpublication@gmail.com

GLOBALISATION AND RURAL DEVELOPMENT

First Published 2007

ISBN 978-81-89886-41-7
(Price: Rs. 380/- INR)

PRINTED IN INDIA

Published by J.K. Singh for Abhijeet Publications, Delhi-110 094, Lasertypeset by Gaurav Graphics, New Delhi and Printed at Himanshu Printers, Delhi.

Dedicated

to

My Parents

M. Sengamalam

&

M. Kamalam

Preface

India entered the era of globalisation in 1990s and how the free and open door investment helps the poors continue to afford in the path of economic progress. The fruits of economic reforms can be enjoyed by all the sections of the people preferably in the rural far-flung areas.

The book attempts to trace the growth and progress of rural areas like Lead Bank Scheme, by service area approach and so on. In a crux, it is the elaborate and concise measures of measuring the rural development. There is a general belief that economic reform and globalisation have improved the status of masses in India but the fruits of LPG have not been yielded any better result to the neglected society.

S. DHARMARAJ

Acknowledgements

I am extremely thankful to T.A. Julius, Former Head of the Department of Economics, Nehru Memorial College, Puthanampatti for his support and encouragement throughout for writing this book.

I owe my sincere thanks to R. Manimekalai, Head of the Department in Economics, Nehru Memorial College, Puthanampatti for her timely help.

I am greatly indebted to Dr. V. Selvaraj, Reader in Commerce, Nehru Memorial College, Puthanampatti for his constant encouragement.

My special thanks to Dr. D. Kumar, Department of Economics, Jamal Muhammad College, Tiruchirapalli, Dr. S. Murugan, Department of Economics, EVR College, Tiruchirapalli and Mr. K. Palanivel, Prof. EVR College, Tiruchirapalli for helping me in all matters of the book information.

I take this opportunity to express my heartfelt thanks to my beloved colleagues P. Rasamahendran, Mr. M.R. Karuppaiah, A. Shanmugam, Dr. V. Murugesan for their constructive criticism in this work.

I owe my affectionate thanks to my beloved friends Mr. A. Sekar, Mr. K. Thiagarajan, Mr. V. Senthil Kumar for their enthusiastic help.

I feel happy to thank my in-laws Mrs. & Mr. A. Eswaran and Mrs. and Mr. Lakshmi Narayanan Software Engineer, Hyderabad, Mr. Murugapandian, Project Manager, Chennai and Mrs. E. Maithili, Lecturer Computer Science S.A. Engineer College, Chennai.

Without their constant pressure and cooperation, I would not have visited centres of learning for data collection.

I will be failing in my duty if I could express my profound thanks to my wife Mrs. Lalitha senior Lecturer in Chemistry, M.A.M. College of Engineering, Tiruchirapalli and to my sons Keerthivasan and Thiru Srinivasan for their timely help in bringing this book in time.

My profound thanks to my beloved sisters Jayalakshmi Muthukannu, Bhagyalakshmi and Umarani who helped me in many ways.

I owe my sincere thanks to my mentor Mr. S. Palanimuthu, M.A., B.Ed. (Retd. Teacher) and Mrs. Kamatchi for the moral support and financial support to take up this project.

I am thankful to Abhijeet Publications, Delhi for their interest and cooperation in publishing this book.

S. DHARMARAJ

Contents

1

Economic Reforms and Rural Development

Issues, Strategies, and Tasks Ahead

It was the early nineties, when India was passing through an unprecedented economic crisis, following political instability that was further aggravated by the impact of the Gulf-War. Our country was trapped in galloping inflation, stress on balance of payment, frustrating position of foreign exchange reserves, and other micro-economic imbalances. To overcome this situation, Dr. Manmohan Singh, the then Finance Minister, introduced the New Economic Policy in the 1991-92 Union Budget. Several policy measures, popularly known as Economic Reforms, were initiated to revive the Indian Economy. Economic reforms set the stage for gradual liberalization and globalization, to reinvigorate the economy and to reap the benefits of worldwide moves in these directions. These reforms were introduced, first as a part of stabilization policy and later to bring in structural adjustment. Stabilization of the economy was important to correct the distortions in key economic areas, but more far reaching results could come only from structural reforms in the economy. These reforms were directed more or less in a sequential order: first to industrial, then foreign trade and financial Sectors.

This new economic policy certainly had direct and indirect impacts on agriculture and rural development in the country. Exclusion of agriculture in any serious discussion on structural reforms in the developing countries is indefensible. It is the largest private sector in the developing economies; it produces tradable goods; agricultural producers respond accordingly to economic signals.

The Macro Scene

Reforms in agricultural scenario in India have been slow and cautious for several reasons. Majority of the farmers in our country cultivate in marginal and small holdings having holding a size less than two hectares. Their dependence on the market for procurement of inputs and for the sale of produce is insubstantial. Markets play a very meagre role in this context, since the strategic objectives related to these sections of farming community are the expansion of their marginal production base, raising productivity of existing resource base and in all providing them with alternative sources of livelihood by protecting them from risks and uncertainties. Secondly, for a large and poor country such as India food security considerations weigh heavily in determining agricultural policies. Comprehensive reforms, which may jeopardize the prospects of food security for the rural and urban poor even in the short-run, will not be accepted with ease. Finally, the complacent attitude of policy makers, reinforced with the over-emphasis on the objective of reducing fiscal deficit as a part of the reform package, led to a continuous decline in the public investment for capital formation in agriculture as well as in the share of the priority sector fending by public sector banks in the 90s.

However, the policy changes at the macro level and those instituted at the sectoral level seem to have made some impact on agricultural growth, but importantly on the dynamics of production relation. The impact may be discussed at two levels. Firstly, the impact of macro policy reforms, especially the attempts to curtail budgetary deficits and realign the value of domestic currencies on agricultural sector, could be looked into. Secondly, we may examine the impact of sectoral policies addressed to agriculture. The latter would include agricultural price policies subsidy policies, trade policies, credit policies, etc. These two sets of impacts are overlapping. Our main attention, however, is on the second aspect of economic policies, i.e. the sectoral policies in agriculture, which in turn affects rural development.

Impact of Economic Reforms on Indian Agriculture and Rural Development

The economic reforms largely focused on fiscal adjustment, foreign trade and investment, industry and financial sectors. Some of the measures, notably reduction of subsidies, reduction of bank lending for priority sector, tariff reductions and trade liberalization do have some impact on agriculture. Agricultural subsidies, which had been provided for agricultural input in the form of minimum support price (MSP) to give favorable and reasonable price to the farmers, have been either reduced or withdrawn completely. Due to total decontrol of potash and phosphate fertilizers, use of these two fertilizers have been almost doubled. Moreover, there is a 30 per cent price hike of nitrogenous fertilizers, which is the result of partial reduction of subsidy in nitrogenous fertilizers. In India, where more than 70 per cent farmers have small and marginal land holding, cannot afford to buy potash and phosphate fertilizers in required amount that resulted in imbalanced fertilizer application. It has a deleterious effect on soil structure and composition that ultimately hampers sustainable agricultural production (Raju and Chowdhry, 1997).

Indian agriculture was characterized by low and stagnant growth performance till the mid-sixties. However, after Green Revolution, the performance improved till the end of eighties (Table 1). Though the other sectors have recorded high growth rates in the 80s as well as the 90s, in their case also, there was no significant difference in performance over two decades. A distinguishing feature in the case of agricultural output is sharp year-to-year fluctuations. Theses high variations imply unpredictable nature of agriculture in India and the precariousness of our food security position. The share of agriculture in GDP is declining steadily; still it continues to contribute nearly one-fourth of the country's GDP (Table 2).

Nevertheless, it is interesting to note that agriculture's share in workforce, particularly in rural areas, is not declining despite its declining importance in the country's GDP. This indicates that more and more people are depending on agricultural activities. It also suggests low absorption capacity of the secondary and tertiary sectors.

In the banking sector, the lending for priority sector has been suggested to reduce from 40 per cent to 10 per cent and gradually phased out by the Narsimhan Committee. The committee has also recommended phasing out of concessional rates of interest on priority sector loans. Moreover, in the name of efficiency and viability, the bank branches in rural areas, which were serving the rural poor peasants and poorer section of the society, are being closed down. Similarly, a number of Regional Rural Banks (RRBs) have also been closed. This would reduce the amount of loans being extended to agriculture and rural development. But, rapid growth of agriculture and non-agricultural segment of rural economy will seek a larger flow of institutional credit. Banking and cooperative credit agencies have to gear themselves up to meet this difficult challenge.

The export thrust of the new economic policies has also accelerated the cropping pattern shifts which results in decline in the area under food grains in favor of exportable or import substitute crops during the post reform period. Consequently, the growth in food grains has fallen short of population growth for the first time since 1975 (Table 3). The benefits from the export-oriented policies do not seem to have reached all sections of the farming community. While the large farmers and reaping the benefits of the policies, small and marginal farmers are languishing for want of resources such as water, and limited access to capital.

The preceding discussion brings out some interesting aspects of recent policy changes. The main macro policy impact on agriculture is the shift in terms of trade in favour of agriculture. It has also resulted in the enhanced market sensitiveness of the producers. However, absence of continuity in policies (especially pertaining to agricultural trade) has increased the market induced risk and uncertainty. The small and marginal farmers are lured by market signals, but they do not have the strength to deal with the market risks. Their problems are aggravated with declining public investment in agriculture.

The small and marginal farmers, who do not possess the wherewithal i.e. access to capital and hence other resources including water, to face the market, have to fend for themselves. The plight of the small and marginal farmers is becoming increasingly serious in the and arid semi-and regions. Which had been even previously neglected by the State. Agriculture producers in these neglected regions are now faced with degraded environment, poor resource base and unfriendly institutional environment. Under these conditions, market penetration in recent years has increased the concentration of scarce resources in fewer hands leading not only to increasing inequalities but also pushing the poor farmers to the edge.

Privatization, as a part of economic reforms, seems to have a negative impact as far as services to the people are concerned. For example, the privatization of rural transportation will naturally cause great inconvenience to people. No private company would like to ply buses in the rural areas, as it would bring them losses. Similarly, privatization has been advocated in education and health sector too. Privatization of these two may only cater to the need of richer sections and a vast majority of people who are poor will be denied access to quality education and health.

Issues To Be Addressed

1. Will not the stabilization aspect of reform measures, which suggests curtailment of public expenditures, withdraw of subsidies and shut down of unprofitable public units have important repercussions on rural employment income and welfare of the poorer sections of the society?
2. Protection of farmers' rights in production, marketing and sale of products.
3. What measures are to be taken exclusively for the backward sections to improve their efficiency?
4. Will the benefits of the new economic policy, which assume rapid economic growth, reach the large masses of poor people?
5. Can growth in agriculture be achieved with a large number of poor farmers with little infrastructural and credit facilities?

Strategies for the Future

1. A multi-agency approach in agriculture and rural development is crucial for its development. Public, private, NGOs, Farmers' organizations must act with better cooperation and coordination
2. People's participation in decision-making regarding planning development process and technology choice is very important to adopt appropriate technology and to improve the development process.

3. Capacity building in the poorer sections of the society by skill training and upgradation.
4. Promote private sector participation in agriculture through contract farming.
5. Priority should be given to evolve location specific and economically viable technologies, for example, region specific improved varieties of agricultural and horticultural crops, and local knowledge based technologies for rural development.
6. Initiation of farming system research which integrates all the factors of production, viz., land., water, labour, capital, and all farm activities such as crop production, livestock rising, dairying sericulture, fisheries, social forestry etc., together to develop a whole farm production system.
7. In the economic reforms area, when lending to the priority section has been reduced, group approach of credit lending may be increased. Micro-financing, supposed to be the better option for credit supply to the peasant and rural artisans, because of in-group landing participants would be more accountable than individual lending. Recent NABARD experiences show a healthy picture regarding repayment capacity of the Self Help Groups (SHGs) particularly women SHGs.

Approaches to Combat Adverse Effects of Economic Reforms on Rural Development

Economic reforms seem to have a negative impact on small and marginal agricultural producers, rural industries, as well as on employment opportunities for the poorer sections of the society. At the moment, when our country has no option other than opening up national economy, the focus should be on adopting the following approaches to mitigate adverse impact of globalization and liberalisation.

1. Generation of appropriate technologies rather than high technologies

Many people consider appropriate technology as traditional or old and thus primitive. This is not true. Appropriate technology means a low cost technology using mainly local or easily available materials and skills to meet a recognized need (Kumar and Hansra, 2000). We can call it intermediate technology. It refers to such small scale technologies emerging out of a gradual process of technology innovations sustainable for the rural poor. The main features of appropriate or intermediate technology are—

a. Need based
b. Self reliant
c. Poor oriented
d. People centered
e. Employment generating
f. Eco-friendly and socio-cultural specific.

Such technologies are more natural, non-polluting and can be locally owned and produced in small units. This would help in avoiding pitfalls of high technologies especially exploitation of natural and human resources.

2. *Participation of local people in planning any developmental activity*

We have experience from our earlier efforts on rural development that the planning process of any development activity starts from the top level. The people, for whom it means have not been consulted in past. Time has come for active participation of the people who are the center of focus of any development process. Agricultural Technology Management Agency (ATMA) is the right initiation towards involvement of the local people in the decision-making process of any development activity of the area. Decentralization of power to Local Self-Governance would be the next step towards this director.

3. *Encourage contract farming to boost agricultural production*

In the present situation, contract farming is viewed as an important tool to increase private corporate involvement in agro-processing and help augment rural employment (Gyotam 2002), Presently, companies engaged in agro-processing and marketing are entering into contract farming by providing farmers with inputs and then buy back the product with a rate specified in advance. A company in contract farming normally provided the following inputs—

a. Required seed variety for cultivation

b. Guidelines to grow the crop

c. Recommended dose of pesticides and fertilizers with no or less residual toxicity

d. Free extension services

e. Other materials if not available locally.

This system would help in eliminating the presence of middlemen and bring the producers and processors in close contact. Farmers can get advantages in terms of assured market, access to technology, timely supply of inputs and more accountable extension services.

4. Participatory technology development

Limitations of new agricultural technology bring about the concept or Participatory Technology Development (PTD) that better suited capable to solve the production problems. It is an alternative approach to develop useful technologies. PTD is the process of bringing together the local communities in one platform with the researchers and other professionals. It requires respect for Indigenous Technical Knowledge (TK) embedded in local society. PTD helps in systematic farm-based research by the local people who face the real problem. This approach will certainly accelerate the adoption process by local masses.

5. Farming System Research and Extension

Farming System Research and Extension is farmer-oriented, problem solving, comprehensive, interdisciplinary, complementary, interactive, and dynamic and responsible society. This approach envisages the whole farm activity by integrating all the factors of production namely, land, water, family labour, and capital. Here the main emphasis is on the collective operation of agricultural, livestock raising, fisheries, sericulture, and social forestry which are complementary to each other. This will not only increase farm income but will also improve employment opportunities to the farming families.

REFERENCES

1. Bhagwati, J (2001). Growth, Poverty and Reforms, *Economic and Political Weekly,* March 10.
2. Government of India, (Ministry of Finance), Economic Survey, Various Issues.
3. Mishra, S.K. & Puri, V.K. (2001). *Indian Economy,* Himalaya Publishing House, Mumbai-400 004.
4. Nagarajan, R. (1997). What Has Happened since 1991? Assessment of India's Economic reforms; *Economic and Political Weekly,* November 8.
5. Raju, S.S. and Chowdhry, K.R. (1997) New Economic Policy and its impact on Rural Development. In *New Economic Policy and Perspective to Rural Development,* Ed. R.P. Singh. NIRD, Hyderabad.
6. Vyas, V.S. (1996). Agricultural Trade Policy for Nineties: Issues and Approaches. *Economic and Political Weekly,* Vol. 29, No. 26, pp. A54-64.
7. Vyas, V.S, (2001). Agriculture: second Round of Economic Reforms, *Economic and Political Weekly,* March 10.

2

Impact of Technology on Globalisation

Technological advances have tremendously forstered globalisation. Technology has in fact been a very important facilitating factor of globalisation.

Several technological developments become a compelling reason for internationalisation. Technological break-throughs are substantially increasing the scale economies and the market scale required to break-even.

Global sourcing was encouraged not only by trade liberalization but also by technological development s which reduced transport costs. Advent of containarisation and super tonnage cargo ships drastically reduced transport costs.

Technology monopoly, like possession of patented technology, encourages internationalization because the firm can exploit the respective demand without any competition.

The pace of globalisation has been accelerated by several enabling technologies. Technological revolution in several spheres, like transport and communication, has given a great impetus to globalisation by their tremendous contribution to the reduction of the disadvantages of natural barriers like distance and cost. The IT revolution has made an enormous contribution to the emergence of the global village. The developments in the field of air cargo transportation has fostered globalisation by enabling quick and safe transportation of sensitive goods (like perishables and goods subject to quick changes in fashion/taste). Developments of containerization and refrigeration have also been of high significance. The steep fall in the cost of transportation and communication have considerably accelerated pace of globalisation. All these have contributed to the drastic transformation of the logistical and global distribution of the value chain system. The world-wide web has a stupendous impact on globalisation.

Global Village

Because of the shrinking time and shrinking space thanks to the technological revolution and the disappearing borders thanks to the liberalization and technological factors the world is evolving into a global village, in several respects.

Contacts between the world's people are widening and deepening as natural and artificial barriers fall. Huge declines in transport and communication costs have reduced natural barriers. Shipping is much cheaper: between 1920 and 1900 maritime transport costs fell by more than two-thirds. Between 1960 and 1990 operating costs per mile for the work's airlines fell by 60 per cent.

Communication is also much easier and cheaper.

Between 1940 and 1970 the cost of an international telephone call fell by more than 80 per cent, and between 1970 and 1990 by 90 percent. In the 1980s telecommunication traffic was expanding by 20 per cent a year. The Internet, the take-off point for the information superhighway, was used by 50 million people in 1998, with the number of subscribers tapping into it doubling every year.

Some of the changes in international trade and finance reflect advances in technology. The lightning speed of transaction means that countries and companies now must respond rapidly if they are not to be left behind.

Technological change is also affecting the nature of investment. Previously, high-technology production had been limited to rich countries with high wages. Today technology is more easily transferred to developing countries, where sophisticated production can be combined with relatively low wages.

The increasing ease with which technology can accompany capital across borders threatens to break the links between high productivity, high technology and high wages. Further, the availability of higher levels of technology all over the world is putting pressure on the wages and employment for low-skilled workers.

Who really benefit from the IT and communication revolution?

Financial Dealers are at the pinnacle of connections. Instant communications, free flows of capital and constant updates from around the world enable money markets from London to Jakarta, from Tokyo to New York, to act as a unit in real time.

Multinational Corporation, too are reaming global markets and integrating production, Cross-border mergers and acquisitions (majority-foreign-owned) account for a large chunk of the total foreign direct investment.

NGOs on-line can campaign around the world, with their messages traveling across borders in seconds. Through e-mail and media networks, people are giving their support to associations across borders—from informal networks to formal organizations.

Skilled labour also travels the global village. With Internet access in nearly every country, the highly educated are increasingly on-line and in touch around the world. In 1998 more than 250, 000 African professionals were working in the United States and Europe, Immigrants with skills in computing technologies are in high demand—in the European Union alone, 500,000 information technology jobs go unfilled because of lack of national skills. The United States offers a special visa to professional immigrants to keep high-tech industries staffed.

Unskilled Labour, by contrast, runs up against hurdles. Many families are divided across international borders as a result of the increasingly tight restrictions in the rich countries in the immigration of unskilled labour. Millions of people do not even have passports—difficult to get. In some countries—let along the visas required to travel abroad.

IT and Marketing

Advances in information technology are revolutionalising the modus operandi of marketing and the business system. The business horizon is humming with buzzwords like internet, world wide web (www), cyberspace, information superhighways etc. which are changing the way of contacting customers; order receiving and processing; and networking and integrating business system. The revolutionary changes being ushered in by the internet are indeed exciting.

Technology experts are anticipating that the internet and the w w w would become the centre of commercial universe. Electronic markets will eliminate the need for intermediaries and that direct contact between manufacturer and customer will bring down the cost of transaction and the cost of the final product. The internet has the potential to evolve into an interconnected electronic market place (cyberspace) bringing buyers and sellers together to facilitate commercial exchanges. The internet is fast becoming an important new channel for commerce in a range of business-much faster than anyone who whould have predicted in he past. The opportunities presented by this new channels seem to be readily apparent; by allowing for direct ubiquitous links to anyone anywhere, the internet allows companies build interactive relationships with consumers and suppliers and deliver new products and services at low cost.

Revolutionary changes in information technology have been sweeping across the global business. Developments in telecommunications and information technologies have reduced the barriers to time and place in doing business. It is now possible for customers and suppliers to transact business at any time any part of the globe, without having to come together physically, thanks to the developments in optical fiber technology, videophone and teleconferencing facilities. The net has changed face and pace of business to business marketing and retailing.

Effective use of information technology helps a company to identify ad profile customers, reach out to customers quickly and more effectively, and make inventory management and distribution system more efficient.

If Indian firms do not keep pace with such contemporary developments, global business, and even domestic business in due course, will be largely out of their reach.

IT has been significantly transforming the distribution system. Xavier points out that effective use of IT in distribution can help companies.

- Reduce inventories
- Reduce delivery time/unproductive waiting time
- Reduce stock-outs/lost sales
- Respond faster to market changes
- Reduce rush orders
- Cut down overproduction
- Reduce unnecessary movement (forwarding and back-tracking)
- Reduce paper-work and wasteful processing
- Plan production better.

All the above benefits result in improved service at a lesser cost. In the West, IT is drastically changing the distribution systems. Electronic networking has become all pervasive. The boundary of the organization is blurring, as it becomes more of a network, with electronic links forward into customers, backwards to suppliers and sideways to business partners. Looking at the enormous benefits, one may wonder as to why Indian companies have not computerized their distribution as yet.

As Xavier points out, IT has also greatly contributed to the retail revolution, which is weeping the entire world. What used to be a fragmented industry has got consolidated du9e to the sophisticated use of IT systems. Large retail chains are gobbling up small-town retailers. Retailing has now become a global business, thanks to the sophisticated IT systems being used by them. Typically, the retail stores were all along operated by owners, but currently the shift is towards systems-driven stores. The major shifts that are taking place in the retail industry are summarized in Table 1.

Table 1: Retail Revolution

From	*To*
Fragmented	Consolidated
Local	Global
Low Technology use	High Technology use
Owner-operated	Systems-driven
Traders	Retail brand managers
Mass marketing	Individualized relationship customization
Market place	Market space

Retailing in developed markets is increasingly becoming net-tailing or e-tailing. Developing countries will follow the trend sooner or later.

The place in the marketing mix is gradually being replaced by (net) space. The channel system is being drastically restructured. The number of intermediaries is falling. An e-tailor may directly deal with the manufacturer and ultimate buyer. Direct marketing will also get a boost.

A large number of match maker or infomediary has sprung up. Infomediaries can have a beneficial role even when the are established dealers for a product, with no need for the match maker to stock the goods. The match maker model of e-commerce connects buyers on one side with sellers on the other. For example, the Jaldi.com has set up an on-line mall for white goods which enables potential buyers to compare price and features across all brands of white goods. The customer can post an inquiry for a model at the site and all the dealers registered with the net marketer will quote the price for it. The customer can then choose the dealer he wants to buy from. Although the dealer will make the sale to the customer, the net marketer will get a commission from the dealer.

The net facilitates quick, easy and wider reach across the globe both for the seller and buyer. This implies that firms which do not have websites will simply be bypassed by may (in future by most) of the potential customers. E-commerce is becoming more quickly prevalent in business to business marketing.

Information technology is becoming all embracing efficiently networking the whole business system, making a shift from e-commerce to e0-business. E-commerce becomes e-business when a company connects its business system directly to its critical constituencies—customers, employers, vendors and suppliers—via intranet, extranet and over the internet.

When a company has properly linked its business system comprising intranet, extranet and over the internet, when a customer places an order by the internet, it gets communicated to the company, distributors and the bankers. Goods are shipped by distributor on intimation to the company and the banker who will collect the money and credit the supplier. When the stock with the distributor falls to a specified level, the company replenishes it. All the these transactions take placer on the real time.

Transfer of Technology

Technology transfer is the process by which commercial technology is disseminated. This will take the form of a technology. Transfer transaction, which may or may not be a legally binding contract, but which will involve the communication, by the transferor, of the relevant knowledge to the recipient. Among the types of transfer transactions that may be used, the Draft TOT Code by UNCTAD has listed the following.

a) The assignment, sale and licensing of all forms of industrial property, except for trade marks, service marks and trade names when they are not part of transfer of technology transactions;

b) The provision of know-how and technical expertise in the form of feasibility studies, plans, diagrams, models, instructions, guides, formulae, basic or detailed engineering designs, specifications and equipment for training, services involving technical advisory and managerial personnel, and personnel training;

c) The provision of technological knowledge necessary for the installation, operation and functioning of plant and equipment, and turnkey projects;

d) The provision of technological knowledge necessary to acquire, install and use machinery, equipment, intermediate goods and / or raw materials which have been acquired by purchase, lease or other means;

e) The provision of technological contents of industrial and technical cooperation arrangements.

The list excludes non-commercial technology transfers, such as those found in international cooperation agreements between developed and developing states. Such agreements may relate to infrastructure or agricultural development, or to international; cooperation in the fields of research, education, employment or transport.

Broadly, there are two forms of TT, viz., internalized and externalized forms of technology transfer. Internalized forms refer to investment associated TT, where control resides with the technology transferor. The transferor, normally, holding the majority or full equity ownership. Externalized forms refer to all other forms, such as joint ventures with local control, licensing strategic alliances and international subcontracting.

The distinguishing feature between these two

modalities of resource transfer is that in internalized TT, the transferor has a significant and continuing financial stake in the success of the affiliate, allows it to use its brand names and to have access to its global technology and marketing networks, exercises control over the affiliate's investment, technology and sales decisions, and sees the affiliate as an integral part of its global strategy. Externalized forms lack one or all of these features, with repercussions on the TT process. Over time, there array of TT arrangements has diversified and particular modes have also become more flexible. Thus, the dividing lines between externalized and internalized modes are becoming less easy to draw.

Levels of TT

A simplified treatment of the subject would suggest four levels of TT.

Operational Level: At the intermediate level are duplicative skills, which include the investment capabilities needed to expand capacity and to purchase and integrate foreign technologies.

Duplicative Level: At the intermediate level are duplicative skills, which include the investment capabilities needed to expand capacity and to purchase and integrate foreign technologies.

Adaptive Level: At this Technological Self-reliance level, imported technologies are adapted and improved, and design skills for more complex engineering learned.

Innovative Level: This level is characterized by innovative skills, based on formal R&D, that are needed to keep pace with technological frontiers or to generate new technologies.

Channels of Technology Flow

The most important channels for the flow of technology are Foreign Investment and Technology Licence Agreements and Joint Ventures.

Foreign Investment: Traditionally, the flow of technology to developing countries has been an integral part of direct foreign investment. Multinational corporations and other firms have resorted to foreign direct investment for a variety of reasons like protection and development of foreign markets, utilization of local resources (in the host country) including cheap labour, overcoming or lessening of the impact of tariff restrictions and tax laws. The flow of sophisticated technology, in particular, has thus been associated with direct investment.

Technology Licence Agreements and Joint Ventures: Technology transfer has been taking place on a significant scale through licensing agreements and joint ventures. There has been a fairly rapid growth of joint ventures, encouraged by government restrictions on foreign investment and foreign trade or the perceived advantages of such ventures. When foreign capital participation in joint ventures is below 50 per cent, technological agreements assume considerable significance.

Methods of Technology Transfer

Transfer of technology takes a variety of forms developing on the type, nature and extent of technological assistance required. The following are the important methods of technology transfer.

1. *Training or Employment of Technical Expert:* Fairly simple and unattended manufacturing techniques processes, can be transferred by imparting the requisite training to suitable personnel. Alternatively, such technology can be acquired by employing foreign technical experts.
2. *Contracts for Supply of Machinery and Equipment:* Contracts for supply of machinery and equipment, which normally provide for the transfer of operational technology pertaining to such equipment, is often quite adequate for manufacturing purposes not only in small scale projects but also in a number of large scale industries where the nature of technology is not particularly complex.
3. *Licensing Agreements:* Licensing agreements, under which the licensor enters into an agreement with a licensee in another country to use the technical expertise of the former, is an important means for the transfer of technology. Licensing agreements are usually entered into when foreign direct investment is not possible or desirable.
4. *Turnkey Contracts:* Transfer of complex technology often takes place through turnkey project contracts, which include the supply of such services as design, creation, commissioning or supervision of a system or a facility to the client, apart from the supply of goods.

Many times, a combination of two or more of the above mentioned methods is used. Turnkey contracts, obviously, are the most comprehensive of such combinations.

Issues in Transfer of Technology

Cost, appropriateness, dependence and obsolescence are the four important issues associated with the transfer of technology.

In many cases, the developing countries obtain foreign technology at unreasonably high pieces. In a number of cases of foreign direct investment associated with technology transfer, the net outflow of capital by way of dividend, interest, royalties and technical fees has been found to be much high than the corresponding inflow.

The appropriateness of the foreign technology to the physical, economic and social conditions of the developing countries is an important aspect to be considered in technology transfer. It has been argued that there are a large number of cases where the foreign technology transferred has been irrelevant or inappropriate to the recipient county's socio-economic priorities and conditions.

Further, heavy reliance on foreign technology may lead to technological dependence.

It is pointed out that the import of modern sophisticated technology has tended to displace the traditional indigenous technology which have been improved under a different set of policies. The steady streams of new products and processes introduced by multinationals into developing countries has been unfavorable to the promotion of domestic technological capacities and has discouraged local scientists and technicians from devoting themselves to practical development problems. It creates a attitude of subservient dependence, which may inhibit the capacity8 to do even relatively minor adaptive research or to adopt processes which are developed locally.

It has also been observed that there is a tendency to transfer outdated technology to the developing countries. Thus, they would not enjoy the advantages of the latest technology and would still technologically lag behind. It is unfortunate that the owners of modem technology view the developing countries as a means to salvage technology that is obsolescent in the advanced countries, even when they possess more advanced technology.

Promotion and Regulation

Despite the problems or shortcomings of foreign technology, it is widely recognized that if properly regulated and promoted it can play a positive role, particularly in the technologically backward LDCs. The governments of India and a number of other countries have, therefore, taken a number of regulatory and promotional measures to take advantage of foreign technology without sacrificing national interests.

Areas of Regulation

A number of regulatory measures have been taken by different countries to ensure that the t technology chosen is the best available, appropriate to domestic conditions and that indiscriminate and unnecessary import of foreign technology is not undertaken. The following are the aspects of technology commonly regulated.

The Extent ad Terms of Equity Participation: These are generally determined by the priorities of the technology-using industry in the nation's economy, supply conditions of the technology and its type and nature.

Phasing of Domestic Manufacturing: Where foreign technology is employed, many governments, including that of India, insisted that suitable provisions should be made for the training of Indians in the fields of production and management. Further, there should be adequate arrangements for research and development, engineering design, training of technical personnel and other measures for the absorption, adaptaion, and development of the imported technology.

The Appropriateness of the Technology: Permission to import a particular technology is generally based on considerations such suitability of the technology to the socio-economic and ecological conditions in the country and ecological conditions in the county and priority of the technology using industry in the national economy. according to the guidelines issued by the Government of India, the entrepreneurs should, to the fullest extent possible, explore alternative sources of technology, evaluate them for a techno-economic point of view and furnish reasons for preferring the particular technology and source of import.

Payment Terms and Foreign Exchange Outflow: Most governments take measures to ensure that disproportionately high payments are not paid for any technology. Restrictions were imposed also on dividend payments and pricing.

The Government of India's guidelines clearly laid down that there should be no requirement for the payment of minimum guaranteed royalty, regardless of the quantum and value of production.

Restrictive Terms in the Agreement: Technology imports with highly restrictive terms on the importing parties are not generally favoured. For instance, according to the Government of India's policy, to the fullest extent possible, there should be no restrictions on free exports to all countries. Further agreements or clauses which in any manner bind the India party with regard to hue procurement of capital goods, components, spares, raw materials, pricing policy ad selling arrangements should be avoided.

Promotional Measures

To take full advantage of the positive role of foreign technology, it is necessary to take certain promotional measures. These include:

1. Assessing technological requirements of various sectors and identifying areas where foreign technology is required.
2. Dissemination of information in foreign counties regarding foreign investment potentials and scope for technical collaboration in the domestic economy, government policy and regulation in respect of foreign capital and technology, institutional assistance and infrastructure ad other facilities for industrial development. The Indian Investment Centre, established in 1961 has been playing such a role.
3. Provision of advisory services to Indian

entrepreneurs in respect of foreign technology including the techniques ad process of technology transfers.

Conclusion

The natural factors and available technology indicate, normally, the innate potential for development of business/economy of a nation/region. The extent to which this potential is really exploited depends on the economic, social and demographic, and political environments.

Technological developments have been revolutionizing the business scene. They facilitate not only the introduction of new products but also tremendous improvements in the operational efficiency and exciting changes in the modus operandi of business. It implies, inter alia, that even when good demand exists for an old product, adoption of the state of the art technology for the conduct of the business would be necessary for survival.

The information technology has vastly transformed the marketing and the financial markets scenario and has significantly contributed to the globalisation process.

Technology often provides a competitive advantage. Success in may industries has a lot to do with R&D ad innovation. There are many factors which stimulate the innovative drive of a firm. These include the company's own strategy, demanding customers, competition (including threat of substitutes), certain social forces, government policies etc.

There is no guarantee that an innovation will be a commercial success. An innovative product can commercially fail due to various reasons; success presupposes several favourable conditions.

An important strategic issue confronting many firms is whether to be a technology leader or follower there are a number of prerequisites, advantages and disadvantages associated with both.

A company may also source technology externally, like from R&D organizations, other firms (including foreign firms). While sourcing foreign technology, the firm should ensure that the technology it chooses is the appropriate one and should be able to properly absorb the technology. Japanese industry in known for the choice of appropriate technology and improving on them after the absorption.

Government policy sometimes is a very important technological environment. Restrictions on foreign technology, scale of operation, type of the technology etc. very adversely affected the Indian business in the past. The liberalization has significantly improved the situation.

Pros and Cons of Globalisation

While globalisation has several benefits, it has a number of problems.

While developing countries which, in the past, were against globalisation, have wide opened their doors for globalisation, may people in developed countries like USA are angry against their globalisation. American jobs and wage levels are severely affected by the influx of cheap imports and shifting of production to low cost overseas locations. According to Business Week/ Harries poll in early 2000, more than two-thirds of

Americans believe that globalisation drags down U S wages. A strong majority of the Americans feel that trade policies have not adequately addressed the concerns of American workers, international labour standards, or the environment. The important pros and cons of globalisation according to the above survey are the following. Productivity grows more quickly when countries produce goods and services in which they have comparative advantage. Living standards can go up faster.

- Global comports keep a lid on prices, so inflation is les likely to derail economic growth.
- An open economy suprs innovation with fresh ideas from abroad.
- Export jobs often pay more than other jobs.
- Unfettered capital flows give the US access to foreign investment and keep interest rates low.
- The adverse effects of globalisation according to the survey are:
- Millions of Americans have lost jobs due to imports or production shifts abroad. Most find new hobs that pay less.
- Millions of others fear losing their jobs, especially at those companies operating under competitive pressure.
- Workers face pay cut demands from employers, which often threaten to export jobs.
- Service and white collar jobs are increasingly vulnerable to operations moving offshore.
- US employees can lose their comparative advantage when companies build advanced

factories in low-wage countries, making them as productive as those at home.

True, globalisation can benefit the developing countries n several ways. It is, however, apprehended that unregulated globalisation will cause serious problems for developing countries.

The almost universal acceptance of the market economy and the globalisation driven by private enterprise tend to aggravate most of the harmful effects traditionally attributed to neocolonialism.

The global dominance of industries by MNCs is on the increase. Many countries are indiscriminate in liberalizing foreign investment. Pepsi, Coke and "junk foods" are allowed even in countries like China.

A number of countries allow high foreign stake even in industries where that is not really required. This could affect domestic enterprise of developing countries.

There has been a large number of cases of takeover of national firms by foreign firms. In some of these cases, the domestic firms are driven to a situation of having to hand over the majority or complete equity to the foreign partners of joint ventures because of the inability of the Indian partners to bring in additional capital or some other incapability.

Replacement of traditional and indigenous products by modern products, resulting in the ruin of traditional crafts and industries and the livelihood of people in these sectors have also been happening in several countries.

One common criticism has been that the technology

that the MNCs bring in may not be the one suited to the host country but that suits the objectives of the MNC. While this could be more true in the liberalized environment of today, another problem, viz., the dumping of outmoded technology to the developing world is not as valid today as in the past and in future it is likely to the even less valid. In the past, because of the entry restrictions and resultant absence or lack of competition, developing countries could be used as a dumping ground for obsolete products, including technology. The business environment today, however, is vastly different. Because of the competition between MNCs (and national firms) made possible by the dismantling of entry barriers (and freeing of technology imports by national firms and added thrust on R&D by them) technological edge is an important determinant of success. The evolution of the motor car market in India, for example, gives some indication of this.

In a competitive environment, a firm can survive only if it is efficient. Companies all around world, including many large multinationals, have been cutting down the size of their human resources as one of the means of achieving cost efficiency. The problem of over-manning is very severe in the developing countries. Unless these firms get rid of the surplus labour, they can hardly be competitive and successful. That means, the liberalization can succeed only if the economy grows very fast to absorb the displaced labour and the new addition to the labour force.

The developing countries, in general, have been disadvantaged by the international trading system. The adverse terms of trade led to economic loss for the developing countries, in general. The least developed countries have been the most deprived. It may, however, be noted that one of the reasons for the adverse terms of trade of the developing countries is the demand-supply factor. It is also estimated that the least developed countries stand to lose up to $600 million a year and sub-Saharan Africa $ 1.2 billion as a result of the Uruguay Round Agreement, while the developed countries are expected to gain very substantially. Multilateral trade liberalizations were mostly in respect of goods traded between industrial economies and those exported from developing to the developed nations did not benefit so much. While developed countries face tariffs 30 per cent higher, because tariffs remain high on the goods with greatest potential for the poorest countries, such as textiles, leather and agricultural commodities.

It should, however, be noted that a number of developing countries have improved their export performance substantially and several of them figure in the list of the top 20 exporters.

Despite the different problems and discriminations, there are chances of developing countries benefiting from trade. "Basic trade theory argues that poor people gain from trade liberalization. Developing countries have a comparative advantage in abundant, low-cost, unskilled labour. If they concentrate on goods shoes production is simple and labour intensive, greater integration into global markets should increase their exports and output, raising the demand for unskilled labour and raising the incomes of the poor relative to those of the non-poor.

Moreover, countries move up the trade ladder,

exporting more sophisticated products, leaving space on the ladder below for later-industrialising countries. All this helps reduce poverty. The countries on the higher rungs benefit most, but even those on the lower rugs should see poverty fall. And free trade should also help poor consumers-without trade protections, local prices should fall to world prices.

There should also be benefits for employment from a liberal financial regime. Removing restrictions on capital flows should attract more FDI, creating more jobs for the poor by integrating them into international systems of production.

It is criticized that developed nations receive most of the FDI. A very small number of the developing countries, which are the relatively developed or large or fast growing in the developing world account for the lion's share of the FDI flows to this cater gory. What the critics do not appreciate is that, as foreign investment flows are based on economic rational it is unrealistic to expect the pattern of flow to be different.

Another criticism is that the liberalization increases the economic inequality. Even in China, the liberalization has created many islands of affluence. If inequality increases because of the worsening of the living conditions of the poor, it certainly is unjustifiable. But, if the increase in inequality is the result of improving the economic conditions of a section, while there is no economic deterioration of ay section, or because of the disproportionate benefits, the question is whether the economic progress of some sections should be curbed so that there will not be a widening of the inequality.

The liaberalisation may increase inequality. Further,

several sectors and sections may not directly and immediately benefit from mere liberalization. There may also be shocks and other adverse effects on the weaker sections. It is, therefore, necessary that there should be real socioeconomic reforms rather than mere liberalization. Targeted poverty eradication programmes and social safety net are very important.

The fast growth ad overall development resulting from liberalization could have a major impact on poverty. Naisbitt points out that there were an estimated 200 to 270 million Chinese living in absolute poverty in 1978 (the year in which the liberalization began) and their number came down to 100 million by 1985. foreign capital has significantly boosted investment and economic growth in China. China has leaped forward on the exports from China. Other counties which carry out proper reforms in real earnest should also be expected to reap such gains in varying degrees. But, half-hearted and confused measures and implementation problems may create more problems than they solve.

Although the MNCs, by the virtue of their size and resources, have certain advantages they may also have limitations or disadvantages in certain spheres or aspects of business. Small and medium firms often have some edge over the very large ones in respects of standardized products or technologies like greater flexibility and adaptability, lower overheads, intimacy with the customers, etc. lower costs is a great advantage which firms from developing countries enjoy. It may be noted that the more component of growth of several India pharmaceutical firms is the foreign market. They are relying mostly on bulk drugs and generics.

What is often ignored while discussing the impact of the product patent is that patented drugs account for only about 15 per cent of the India drug market. There are several more products which would go off patent in the coming years which can also be taken up the India firms. The new patent and thereby enabling Indian firms also to develop patented products. Positive signs are already there on the horizon.

There are also many evidences of the better technology brought in by the MNCs inducing or provoking Indian firms to absorb similar technology leading to their enhanced competitiveness and market expansion.

Policy Options

With a view to minimizing the damages and maximizing the opportunities of globalisation from the macro socioeconomic point of view, the Human Development Report 1997 of the UNDP has made to following policy suggestions.

1. Manage trade and capital flows more carefully.
2. Invest in poor people.
3. Foster small enterprises.
4. Properly manage new technology.
5. Reduce poverty and introduce safety nets.
6. Influence governance.

The Report also points out that to seize the opportunities of globalisation, the poorest developing countries need the following.

1. A more supportive macroeconomic policy

environment for poverty eradication. The world clearly needs much more effective macroeconomic policy management at the global level with more stable sources of international liquidity, better surveillance, faster crisis response mechanisms and a larger multinational lender of last resort. Existing organizations serve these purposes inadequately.

2. A fairer institutional environment for global trade. There is an urgent need to treat the products of developing countries on a par with those of industrial countries and to accelerate the liberalization of markets of interest to poor countries, such as textiles, and institute a comprehensive ban on dumping agricultural exports.

3. A partnership with multinational corporations to promote growth for poverty reduction. An incentive system that, while avoiding excessive regulation, encourages multinational corporations to contribute ot poverty reaction and be publicly accountable and socially responsible. Both industrial and developing countries have interests here. Those of the industrial include preventing tax evasion.

4. Action to stop the race to the bottom. In a world of cutthroat competition, countries underbid each other in labour costs, labour standards and environmental protection-to produce as cheaply as possible for the international market. Many countries unilaterally try to restrain these races to the bottom. And some may come under external pressure if they tolerate dangerous working conditions ad child labour, with human rights issues a basis for unilateral trade sanctions. A more efficient and equitable approach would be to strengthen institutions such as the international Labour

Organisation –to support respect for labour right – and to develop similar institutions for international environmental protection. International coordination is also needed to avoid races to attract international investors by offering overly generous tax incentives that erode the tax base.

5. Selective support of global technology priorities.

6. Action on global debt. The highly indebted poor countries need debt relief now – not at some indeterminate point in the future. Providing effective relief to the 20 worst-affected countries would cost between $ 5.5 billion and $ 7.7 billion – less than the cost of one Stealth bomber and roughly equivalent to the cost of building the Euro-Disney theme park in France.

Globalisation of Indian Business

India's economic integration with the rest of the world was very limited because of the restrictive economic policies followed until 1991. Indian firms confined themselves, by and large, to the home market. Foreign investment by Indian firms was very insignificant.

With the new economic policy ushered in 1991, there has, however, been a change. Globalisation has in fact become buzz-word with Indian firms now, and many are expanding their overseas business by different strategies.

This section takes a look at the hurdles to and prospects for globalisation of Indian business and the different globalisation strategies.

Obstacles To Globalisation

The Indian business suffers from a number of disadvantage in respect of globalisation of business. The important problems are the following.

Government Policy and Procedures: Government policy and procedures in India are among the most complex, confusing and cumbersome in the world. Even after the much publicized liberalization, they do not present a very conducive situation. One prerequisite for success in globalisation is swift and efficient action. Government policy ad the bureaucratic culture in India in this respect are not that encouraging.

High Cost: High cost of many vital inputs and other factors like raw materials and intermediates, power, finance infrastructure facilities like port etc., tend to reduce the international competitiveness of the Indian business.

Poor Infrastructure: Infrastructure in India is generally inadequate and inefficient and therefore very costly. This is a serous problem affecting the growth as well as competitiveness.

Obsolescence: The technology employed, mode and style of operations etc., are, in general, obsolete and these seriously affect the competitiveness.

Resistance to Change: There are several socio-political factors which resist change and this comes in the way of modernization, rationalisation and efficiency improvement. Technological modernisation is resisted due to fear of unemployment. The extent of excess labour employed by the Indian industry is alarming.

Because of this labour productivity is very low and this in some cases more than offsets the advantages of cheap labour.

Poor Quality Image: Due to various reasons, the quality of many Indian products is poor. Even when the quality is good, the poor quality image India has becomes a handicap.

Supply Problems: Due to various reasons like low production capacity, shortages of raw materials and infrastructures like power and port faculties, Indian companies in many instances are to able to accept large orders or to keep up delivery schedules.

Lack of Experience: The general lack of experience in managing international business is another important problem.

Limited R & D and Marketing Research: Marketing Research and R & D in other areas are vital inputs for development of international business. However, these are poor in Indian business.

Expenditure on R & D in India is less than one per cent of the GNP while it is two to three per cent in most of the developed countries. In 1994-95, India's per capita R & D expenditure was less the $3 when it was between $ 100 and $825 for most of the developed nations. The competition is growing not only from the firms in the developed countries but also from the developing country firms. Indeed, the growing competition from the developing country firms is a serious challenge to India's international business.

3

A New Strategy for IRDP Implementation

India is a country of villages. There are 5,58,989 villages in India. It was therefore felt that the problem of poverty in India could be overcome by attacking rural poverty. The IRDP was introduced as a direct instrument for attacking India's rural poverty which is both extensive and endemic.

In any scheme of development, the opportunities made available are snatched away by the stronger sections in denial of opportunities to the poorest sections of society particularly in rural areas. To ensure that the rural poor are also afforded opportunities for their development a specific scheme called 'Integrated Rural Development Programme' (IRDP) was designed. The IRDP seeks, skills, support services and institutional arrangements with the basic objective of enabling them to cross the poverty line through additional employment and income generation.

The IRDP was introduced in certain selected areas of the country in 1978. It was later on extended to the whole of rural India with effect from October 2, 1980. The target group of the IRDP consists of families of small and marginal farmers, agricultural labourers and rural artisans whose income is below the pre-determined poverty line which is presently fixed at Rs. 11,000 per annum.

Under the IRDP acquisition of assets by the poor in the primary, secondary and tertiary sectors, is enabled through financial assistance in the form of credit support by banks and subsidy given by the Government. Normally, subsidy is provided at the rate of 25 per cent of the project cost for small farmers, 33.3 per cent for agricultural labourers, marginal farmers and rural artisans, and 50 per cent to SC/ST.

Performance

Since the launching of the IRDP, bank credit of Rs. 13230 crores and Government subsidy amounting to Rs. 8202 crores, aggregating to Rs. 21432 crores had been provided to 447 lakh families below the poverty line till the end of the financial year 1994.

There are a number of supporting programmes under IRDP. Training of Rural Youth to Self Employment (TRYSEM), for providing technical assistance to the rural youth in the age group of 18 and 35 years, from the poor families to enable them to take up self employment is one of such schemes, Development of Women and Children in Rural Areas (DWCRA), for focusing attention on women members of such families with a view to providing them with opportunities of self employment is another programme. Other supporting programmes include provision of infrastructure for filling in critical gaps having direct relevance to the beneficiaries.

Notwithstanding the fact that bank credit of Rs. 13230 crores and total subsidy of Rs. 8202 crores were passed on to the beneficiaries, the contribution towards amelioration of the lot of the beneficiaries in question and the overall economic development of rural India was not visible even at the end of 1994, i.e., after 14 years of extension of the scheme to the entire Rural India. The concurrent evaluation of the IRDP for the year 1989 conducted by the Government of India revealed that only in 28 per cent of the cases, old beneficiaries had been able to cross the then existing poverty line of Rs. 6400 per annum. Although the programme had the lofty objective of enabling all rural poor below the poverty line to cross the poverty line, the results achieved are not wholly satisfactory. No doubt the IRDP was ideally tailored to the needs of the poor. Indeed the problem of the poor do match with the professed role of the IRDP in as much as it would provide the assets that the necessary support services to facilitate their productive use.

Defects Galore

However during the actual implementation of the project, several distortions, and administration defects and deficiencies in modalities came to light. Faulty selection of beneficiaries, weak designs of the projects, absence of backward and forward linkages, lack of co-ordination among the key agencies like banks, panchayats, Government departments, and non-governmental organizations, etc., also came to light. Many weaknesses in the administration of IRDP were also found.

Mehta Committee

In November 1993, an expert committee on IRDP was constituted to review the IRDP and to make suitable recommendations to improve matters, Mr. D.R. Mehta, former Deputy Governor, Reserve Bank or India, was the Chairman of the committee. The committee in its report submitted in November 1994, made several recommendations to make the IRDP and its implementation more effective.

For bringing about better involvement of banks in the IRDP implementation, the committee recommended that they may be given freedom at least on a pilot basis for selecting beneficiaries from Below Poverty Line Lists (BPL lists). It also recommended that officers from commercial banks, that officers from commercial banks, NABARD, RRBs, may be inducted into District Rural Development Agencies (DRDAs) to make them compact professional teams of experts. The committee also recommended that the work relating to identification of investment opportunities and preparation of project profiles be undertaken on more professional lines by a district level technical group to be set up by DRDAs.

According to another major recommendation of the committee, banks should consider extending credit fro acquisition of land besides making capital finance available for meeting current expenditure. The committee recommended cash credit facility for non-farm sector also to enable them to meet their working capital requirements. The committee also recommended that both the loan and subsidy provided under IRDP should be suitably enhanced for ensuring higher income generation. Stressing the need for timely recovery of bank loans, the committee recommended the appointment of special recovery officers for banks in each district and utilization Reports-cum-Recovery Facilities on a commission basis at a lower level. For improving infrastructural support, the committee suggested that DRDAs should prepare a perspective plan of infrastructure in consultation with District Consultative Committees taking into account the resource availability and the felt needs of the rural population. According to the committee training should be imparted to rural youth so as to upgrade their skills and make them eligible for assistance under IRDP. Other recommendations of the committee relate to encouragement of group/cluster approach and non farm activities under IRDP and extension of the system of cash disbursement throughout the country.

Remedial Steps

While conveying its acceptance of most of the recommendations made by the committee the Reserve Bank of India in February 1995 advised banks to implement certain recommendations. Banks have been asked to advise their branches to attend meetings conveyed by panchayats to approve BPL list drawn by the block authorities. Banks may provide loans under IRDP for acquisition of land together with short term credit for meeting current farm expenditure. NABARD has been asked to issue guidelines to banks regarding cost of land at various places. Banks were asked to ensure that adequate number of good quality animals as also the required linkages in terms of feed and marketing are available before extending credit for animal husbandry.

Banks have been asked to ensure that the loan components are enhanced suitably to cover project cost minus available subsidy so that the projects undertaken would be of adequate size to generate sufficient income to enable the beneficiaries to go above the poverty line at one go. NABARD was advised to consider revision of economic size of units. Working capital requirements should be fully taken into account while sanctioning loans to the IRDP beneficiaries and suitable cash credit limits sanctioned together with term loans under IRDP, banks may consider sanction of need based working capital limits to the borrowers. For all activities under IRDP upto Rs. 25,000-obtaining mortgage may be dispensed with. However for loans above Rs. 25,000 but upto Rs. 50,000 normal banking norms including mortgage/margin etc., may be followed without asking for any collateral security.

While considering loan proposals to industries service business (ISB), sector under IRDP, banks may keep in mind the need to promote non-farm, tiny/ small enterprises and services sector for creating more employment opportunities. Banks may extend cash disbursement to IRDP beneficiaries subject to the RBI guidelines/conditions prescribed in 1991. Banks may initiate action to provide orientation training to IRDP beneficiaries. Banks may fix realistic repayment schedules after taking into account the level of income generation and economic lift of the assets. The minimum repayment period for IRDP loans be fixed at five years as against the present three years. Initial moratorium may also be provided wherever required. Banks may provide group loans for various activities under IRDP. Such group loans should cover assistance required for infrastructure. The rate of interest and security requirements in such cases would however be related to *per capita* quantum of the loan.

The Lead Bank officers supervise the constitution and working of the Technical group besides maintaining liaison with controlling offices of banks. State Government officials, Panchayat Raj Institutions, Voluntary Organizations (VOs) and Self Help Groups (SHGs) for improving recoveries. The RBI has advised banks that they may obtain services of utilization reporters cum Recovery Facilitators on a contract basis.

Altered Approach

The results to be achieved as a consequence of the implementation of the above instructions of RBI are yet to be seen. In my view, the above instructions of the RBI apart from the present approach of State Governments particularly the District Administration and block level officials to the IRDP implementation should undergo a change. Their present approach is just to protect performance on the basis of data and statistics relating to subsidy utilization without laying any accent on quality of achievement, and generation of income through the pursuit of productive activities by the beneficiaries. The review in District Consultative Meetings, etc., is also confined to subsidy utilization by different banks and the reviews do not go beyond that. Such an approach on the part of the Government has resulted in generation of data regarding performance and not generation of income and creation of productive assets and not real performance leading to alleviation of poverty and overall economic development. Under such an approach, banks do not have any motivation and extend financial assistance under IRDP.

As a matter of fact, banks are thoroughly scared to lend under IRDP. Their fear is that by lending under IRDP they will be creating more and more NPAs in the years to come and it is felt by many banks that by lending as per commitments and targets they are not achieving anything beyond giving "statistical" pleasure and happiness to the district administration. Therefore, to enthuse and motivate banks, government and district administration should change their attitude and their perception of the programme itself. The Government should show more concern and seriousness about the proper and result oriented implementation of IRDP *in lieu* of the present data oriented interpretation.

There is a strong case for such an altered approach. The present system of pursuing and compelling to lend under IRDP as per subsidy targets should be replaced by a system of motivation and real participation of banks as indicated above. More attention should be given for identification and selection of beneficiaries. Only those candidates who are fully motivated to start an activity by taking IRDP loans and those who are confident of making a success and repaying the loans should be selected as beneficiaries. Such an approach will go a long way in creating real economic activities, and in generating income and creating productive assets.

Another way to enthuse and motivate banks is by creating a better atmosphere for recovery. There should be no promise of loan waivers, write offs, etc., anywhere. There should be efforts on the part of all the state Government officials, politicians and the society at large to develop a good payment culture.

Stress in Recovery

The recovery performance in respect of IRDP loans granted by public sector banks as a percentage to demand has declined to 30.87 per cent as at the end of June 1993 from 41.34 per cent as at the end of June 1991. The low recovery of IRDP loans has affected the credibility of the entire programme. Poor recovery of loans hinders effective recycling of funds by banks and consequently they would remain unenthused about enhancing their IRDP loans. If IRDP loans become NPAs banks, do not earn any interest on such loans. On the other hand banks have to make provision for such loans. Therefore, it is essential that state Government and district and block level government authorities should give full assistance and support to banks in the recovery of IRDP loans. The state government should appoint special recovery officers in each district to extent help to banks in the matter of recovery and in development of a good repayment culture, banks will get enthused and motivated to implement IRDP. In the future strategy therefore there should be more stress on recovery of IRDP loans.

The Government may also pass appropriate laws to ensure that defaulters are not allowed to contest elections to panchayats, legislative assemblies, etc. Defaulters should not be permitted to hold any public offices. Loan waivers, waivers of interest or penal interest etc., by the state or Central Governments should be totally stopped. Willful defaulters should not be given assistance under any other scheme. All these efforts will create a better environment for recovery and help build up a good repayment culture in the long term.

Sound Economics

Sound economics alone should play its role and not politics in the matter of implementation of IRDP in future. If this is ensured by all concerned, the IRDP will acquire credibility and it will get implemented on sound and proper lines, thereby contributing to generation of employment opportunities, generation of income, creation of assets and overall economic development.

Therefore, the future strategy for IRDP implementation should be based on motivation of banks through proper and correct selection of beneficiaries and through support in the matter of recovery of loans by the Government and not on the basis of mere targeting for subsidy utilization. In the proposed strategy, the accent should be not an increasing mere quantum of IRDP loans and quantum of subsidy releases, for "statistical" pleasure of district administration and state government, but it should be an extra productive economic activities and extra income and new assets generated through the IRDP. If such a strategy is adopted it will surely contribute to better implementation of IRDP, thereby contributing to the amelioration of the lot of people below the poverty line as well as to the overall economic development.

Mahatma Gandhi had said "Recall the face of the poorest and weakest man whom you may have seen and ask yourself if the step you contemplate is going to be of any use to him...". The state Governments and district administration should therefore ask themselves whether the mere release of subsidy and IRDP loans are going to fetch any enduring benefit to the people below the poverty line. Therefore in the future strategy the Government and banks should regard the candidate selected for assistance under IRDP not as mere beneficiaries but as entrepreneurs the core of the future strategy should cover intensification of efforts at ensuring that the projects of the beneficiaries under the programme grow as visible units sustainable in the free market which can generate adequate income for the entrepreneurs not only for sustaining themselves, but also to enable them to repay their debts and make above the political line. Such a healthy approach alone can fetch enduring benefits for the beneficiaries thereby leading to real economic development in rural India.

Population and Socio-Economic Development in India

For demographers and economists, the question of the relationship between population growth and development is not a new one. It has been a point of debate for long time as to whether the relationship is positive or negative, whether the population growth deters or promotes development or vice-versa and whether two can ultimately settle down to a point of equilibrium. Opinion has fluctuated between pessimism and optimism. At present, there is also a view with the experiences of some developed countries that the population growth is no more a constraint for economic development.

In spite of the different view points, the fact is

that the population growth is related to the development particularly for the developing countries. This is probably because the population by itself plays a vital role as a producer and a consumer. It is fairly well established fact that in the early stages of economic development role of population can be viewed both as producer and consumer. However, once the development crosses the take off stage, the population is likely to undergo various demographic changes such as size, growth, composition and distribution associated with numerous relevant economic and social variables (UN 1975). The essence of his was captured in the popular slogans at World Population Conference, 1974 in Bucharest, "Development is the best road to slowing population growth" (Bhattacharjee, A., 1993). The term development normally refers to overall improvement on both economic and non-economic structures in an area of observation over time. The economic development mainly represents the growth in agriculture and industries and is normally reflected in the rise of *per capita* income whereas the non-economic development represents the improvement is social factors like education, health, etc., and cultural factors like age at marriage for females or adoption of family planning methods, etc. Further, both economic and non economic factors are inter-mixed and interrelated such that it is difficult to find out the contribution of each single factor in overall development. However, it may be possible to identify a group of various economic and social factors which can be used as an index to measure the economic and social development of an area separately.

India is one such country where various socio-economic development along with major changes in the demographic situation have been taking place and the linkages between population growth and development can be observed at the state level. Therefore, it may be interesting and useful to examine this linkage among the major states in India.

Developments

Indian economy at the time of attaining independence was identified with mass poverty, chronic unemployment and under employment high level of dependent on agriculture and low level of productivity. This is also accompanied by higher population growth with low level education and had health condition. Therefore, overall development and reconstruction of economy were the obvious imperatives in the post-independence period (Agarwal, Verma and Gupta, 1992).

To meet this challenge, different economic policies were initiated since 1951. This has resulted into a tremendous progress in the growth of both agriculture and industrial sectors. The agriculture output recorded an increase of 4 times since 1951. The total food production of about 58 million tones in 1992. Similarly, the industrial output has also recorded an overage growth rate of about 8 percent during this period. The index of industrial production in 1991 is about 980 measured at base of 1951 (1951=100). *Per capita* income at current prices of Rs. 238 in 1951 increased to Rs. 4,250 in 1990. The shares of gross domestic production in primary, secondary and tertiary sector respectively of 56.5,15.0 and 28.5 per cent in 1950-51, had changed to 33.9, 27.0 and 39.1 per cent respectively showing substantial progress.

The population of India increases at the rate of 21.51, 24.80, 24.75 and 23.50 respectively during 1951-61, 1961-71, 1971-81 and 1981-91. The growth rate of population recorded increasing trends Upto the period of 1951-81, and it is only during 1981-91, a decline in the growth rate is observed. This decline in the growth rate is significant and provides a sign of hope in the sense that at least the family planning programme in the country has been able to cross the demographic barriers. During this period, the birth rate is brought down from about 41 to about 29 (R.C. India, 1992). The couple protection rate has increased to about 45 per cent (Government of India, 1992). Similarly, the crude death of 27.4 during 1941-50 declined to about 10 in 1991. The infant mortality rate of about 150 during 1951 declined to about 80 in 1991. There has been a significant rise in the expectation of life at birth for males and females. The expectation of life at birth for males of 32.4 during 1941-51 increased to 58.1 during 1986-91, and the expectation of life at birth for females increased from 31.7 to 59.1 during the same period (Government of India, 1991). Thus, it is clear from the above observation that a major demographic change has taken place in India during the post-independence period.

Over time, significant improvement is made in the field of education and health. The literacy rate of 16.7 per cent (literate to the total population) in 1951 has increased to 52.1 per cent (aged 7 years and above) in 1991. The literacy among the males has increased from 24.9 per cent in 1951 to 63.9 per cent in 1991 and among the females it has increased from 7.9 per cent to 39.4 per cent.

There is also a substantial improvement of the health situation in the country. Since most of our people were used to live in rural areas with inadequate health facilities and other socio economic backwardness, the recommendation was made for establishment of "Primary Health Centers" for every 100,000 population. This was designed to serve as a nucleus for providing some degree of integrated medical service (Banerji, 1973). A large-scale expansion in the health services was made subsequently by establishing large number of PHCs and subcentres with medical and paramedical staff. At present, there are about 33,000 PHCs and 1,30,000 subcentres functioning in the country for providing medical services to the rural people. Along with the improvement of health infrastructure in the rural areas, there has been a significant increase in the establishment of hospitals, nursing homes, polyclinics, diagnostic centers, specialized health units etc., in big cities and urban areas. This has resulted into a substantial decline in the death rate as well as rise in the expectation of life at birth as cited earlier. Thus, it is clear that India had undergone major changes in socio-economic and demographic situation. It can be observed that at national level, the demographic change it is positively associated with socio-economic development. However, this relationship at the aggregate level may not reveal the correct picture at the state level as the achievement of the socio-economic development at state level are different. It may be possible to identify some states with higher level of development associated with lower level of fertility and vice-versa. This identification of the development is done by selecting different variables as follows.

A. Social variables

1. General literacy rate
2. Female literacy rate
3. Age at marriage for female
4. Expectation of life at birth
5. Infant mortality rate
6. Bed population ratio
7. Average *per capita* expenditure on health and education.

B. Economic variables

1. Per capita income
2. Percentage of urban population to the total population
3. Percentage of population below poverty line
4. General activity rate.
5. *Per capita* income from agriculture
6. Bank per one lakh population
7. Registered factories per one lakh population
8. *Per capita* consumption of electricity.

C. Demographic variables

1. Population growth rate
2. Crude birth rate
3. Crude death rate
4. Total fertility rate
5. Couple protection rate
6. Net migration rate.

Classification of States according to the Level of Development

As the objective is to compare the level of development between states in India. A composite index is developed by considering various Demographic social and economic variables at a point of time. Since the data for most of the variables are available around 1991, the composite index thus computed would refer for 1991. The value of each variable is converted into a common (0-100) scale, with the lowest value as zero and the highest as 100 when the variables is positively associated and with the highest value of the variables as zero and the zero and the lowest as 100 when the variable in inversely associated. The intermediate values of the variables are estimated by simple interpolation. The average of the total score thus obtained for different states would determine the relative position of a particular state among the states selected for measuring the level of development (McGranahan, 1972). The composite index for social and economic development also computed separately.

According to the composite index for social development, the most socially advanced state is Kerala and this is followed by Punjab, Maharashtra and Tamilnadu. The most socially backward state is Madhya Pradesh and is followed by Uttar Pradesh, Bihar and Rajasthan. Similarly, according to the composite index for economic development, the most economically advanced state is Punjab and is followed by Gujarat, Maharashtra and Haryana.

The most economically backward state is Bihar and is followed by Orissa, Assam and Uttar pradesh. If, both social and economic development are combined the composite index reveal an interesting picture in the sense that by and large the social development and economic development are interrelated in the status of the states. Accordingly, it can be observed from Table 4, that eight states which have higher values of composite index than the national average are identified as developed states. They are Punjab, Kerala Maharashtra, Tamilnadu, Karnataka, Haryana and West Bengal. The other states, viz., Bihar, Madhya Pradesh, Uttar Pradesh, Rajasthan, Assam, Orissa and Andhra Pradesh can be identified as underdeveloped states in India.

Relationship between Development and Demographic Changes

As mentioned earlier, the socio-economic development and demographic change are linked by a chain of inter-dependent variables. In demographic change, population growth is due to balance of natural increase and migration. In socio-economic term development is dependent upon technological advanced in industry, transportation, agriculture, education, health and medicine apart from its effect in the natural increase of population. This development also has created various opportunities for migrants which in turn affected population growth particularly at the state level. Thus, the relationship between socio-economic development at the state level should be viewed through the index of fertility and not by the population growth index to access the impact of development on demographic changes.

The states which are identified as socially advanced states have lower CBR and also lower CDR, than the national average of CBR and CDR.

GLOBALISATION AND DECENTRALISED DEVELOPMENT

The economic crisis mainly consisting of foreign exchange crisis and shortages of supply necessitated the introduction of economic reforms in the middle of 1991. These reforms had three major components, namely, Globalization, Liberalization and Privatization.

The Globalization part is expected to ensure enlarged competitive environment with its attendant backward and forward linkages which are necessary for the opening of the economy, flow of foreign capital and multifaceted technology transfer and access to overseas markets. Globalization also ensures transparency, flow of information and access to data and other information to one and all.

The concept of decentralization is widely accepted and debated but needs to be emphasized because more economic powers are needed for specific sectoral (area and product) development. Decentralization must also cover the economic decision-making process at the local levels so that too much bureaucratic controls may be removed which come in the way of the development of potentially feasible growth centers, hitherto bogged down by the political, bureaucratic and such other obstacles.

Pranab Bardhan, (1996), in his paper on decentralized development, defines decentralization in the sense of political decision making power from mere administrative delegation of functions of the Central Government to local agencies. Local accountability is essential in decision making and its implications. In support of his case for economic decentralization, he quotes the World Bank data for forty two developing nations which reveals that where the maintenance of roads was decentralized, the condition of roads were found much better than in centrally managed systems of road maintenance. According to him, the data for another group of developing nations reveals that the per capita costs of water in World Bank funded projects are four times higher in centralized than in fully decentralized system.[1]

This article attempts to highlight and argue in favour of a systematic change that aims at bringing about certain types of developments where government's approach has failed but can be turned around with the new experiment—whereby in a globalize economy, the government agencies and Non-Governmental Organizations (NGOs) work in tandem for a speedier breakthrough in specified areas of rural development such as cattle development, horticulture, floriculture, food-processing industry and afforestation etc. for this, it would be necessary to have decentralization of economic decision-making power so that the delays may be avoided due to centre-state-local government channelisation.

Shikha Jha, (2002)[2], evaluates the efforts towards strengthening rural governments in India through rural decentralization process initiated with the 73rd Constitutional Amendment Act, 1992. She concludes that fiscal decentralization is a welcome step indeed but it is only the first step towards achievement of fiscal autonomy should be greater public participation so that the fiscal operations of Panchayati Raj Institutions become more transparent, responsible and accountable.

Arguing in favor of decentralized government with

multi-level planning and multi-level public finance in the country. M.A. Oommen, (2001), has quoted a calculation by the National Institute for Rural Development (NIRD), whereby, based on certain physical norms, unit cost inflation rate and so on, the capital and operation and maintenance (O & M) cost for drinking water supply, rural sanitation, street lighting, primary education, primary health care and rural roads, all of which are considered as core basic services, for five years (2000-05). It comes to Rs. 22,731 crore. He is of the view that the Panchayati Raj Institutions cannot be expected to raise even a small part of this resource.[3]

However, in view of the resource crunch faced by the state governments all over the country, the desired degree of success would continue to elude us. This strengthens the case for the involvement of NGOs further in the gigantic task of rural development.

Government-NGO Interface

There is a strong case for interface between Government agencies and the NGOs as the new economic reforms have coincided with a conscious effort at political decentralization through the 73rd and 74th Constitutions Amendments. In the changing scenario, despite several claims by the government agencies, much has not changed at the grass-roots level. There is an urgent need for decentralization of economic decision-making power.

The steps taken by the government on the political front are welcome, but at the same time, it is necessary to establish greater coordination between the

Table 1 : Size of holding-wise distribution of beneficiaries according to Broad Household Income Groups

Size of Holding Groups(Hectares)	*Upto 20,000*		*20,000 to 40,000*		*40,000 to 60,000*		*60,001 to 100,000*		*Abov 100,000*		*Total*		*Average Per Households*
	(a)	*(b)*	*(a)*	*(b)*	*(a)*	*(b*	*(a)*	*(b)*	*(a)*	*(b)*	*(a)*	*(b)*	*(Rs.)*
Non-Cultivators	-	-	3	100.00	-	-	-	-	-	-	3	100.00	29,333
Marginal (Upto 1.00 ha)	5	35.7	4	28.6	2	14.3	3	21.4	-	-	14	100.00	35,571
Small (1.01-2.00 ha)	-	-	2	12.5	5	31.3	9	56.2	-	-	16	100.00	56,250
Medium (2.01-4.00 ha)	-	-	-	-	3	23.1	8	61.5	2	15.4	13	100.00	78,923
Large (above 4.01 ha)	-	-	-	-	-	-	2	50.0	2	50.0	4	100.00	1,11,250
Total	5	10.0	9	18.0	10	20.0	22	44.0	4	8.0	50	100.00	59,140

N.B. a) No. of Households

b) Percentage of Households to total in each holding group (row-wise)

Source : Ahmad Noman S. *Rapid Rural Transformation Through Voluntary Action*, M.D.Publications Pvt. Ltd., New Delhi 1997.

government agencies and the NGOs at the grass-roots level for rapid rural transformation.

Despite serious efforts and best intentions, the government agencies fall to deliver the goods on the ground as they prefer to do things for the people rather hand encouraging them to do things for themselves and help them become self-reliant.[4]

Several arguments are put forward in favour of decentralization. However, decentralization alone does not work and some form of interface between the government agencies and the NGOs becomes necessary. The ultimate responsibility or accountability rests with the Government as far as development of the people is concerned be it economic, social or cultural. Therefore, the central control of the government is necessary. It is important to design mechanisms of coordination or interface between government agencies and the NGOs.

Table 2 : Percentage Distribution of Income by Main Sources

Size of Holding Group	*No. of Families*	*Source of Income*			
		Agriculture	*Dairying*	*Other*	*Total*
Non-cultivator (Nil)	3	-	95.5	4.5	100.00
Marginal	14	19.0	74.4	6.6	100.00
Small	16	24.8	65.7	9.5	100.00
Medium	13	44.1	55.9	-	100.00
Large	4	70.1	29.9	-	100.00
Total	50	36.0	59.6	4.4	100.00

Source : Ahmad Noman S., *Rapid Rural Transformation Through Voluntary Action*, M.D. Publication Pvt. Ltd., 1997, p. 73.

A Success Story

The dramatic success story of an NGO in the forefront in Pune District of Maharashtra has important lessons for the theory of rural economic development through NGO involvement, it is the case study of Bharatiya Agro-Industries Foundation (BAIF).[5] Since its establishment, BAIF has made exemplary contribution in the field of rural development and has been appreciated at different levels, including the government. Since it combines research and development, it is called BAIF Development and Research Foundation.

The BAIF recognizes the rural family as the most important unit in the development of rural areas it adopts a holistic approach towards rural development. It aims to supplement incomes of the rural households, generate gainful employment and an improved quality of life by using locally available resources and the programmes are implemented with professional outlook and scientific support.

The BAIF ensures that the programme is economically viable and does not compete with the Government or any other agency in the same area.

The cattle development programme in the selected region has shown excellent results not only in the livestock sector but in the overall rural transformation. The income of the beneficiary group (consisting of 50 households) chosen randomly is much higher than the non-benefit (households) chosen randomly is much higher than the non-beneficiary group (also consisting of 50 households) chosen randomly as dairying from crossen randomıy as dairying from cross-bread animals has supplemented the incomes of the beneficiaries.

As stated by the informants themselves, farm incomes are derived deducting all the expenses, from the gross value of production at farm harvest prices. Incomes from dairying are also derived by similar procedure. The net incomes from other sources are as mentioned by the reporting families. However, the calculation of net incomes has ignored the sophistication of depreciation, land revenue payments etc. The expenses included input costs, wages, maintenance expenses, interest payments etc. However, it serves the purpose of the income status of the beneficiaries.

The annual incomes of beneficiary families are clubbed into five broad ranges taking into account the net incomes accruing from all the sources. Further, the beneficiaries in various income ranges are classified according to their size groups of operational holdings. The relevant data are presented in Table-1.

It may be seen from the table that only 10 per cent of beneficiaries fall in the range of upto Rs. 20,000. All these belong to the marginal holding group. Another 18 per cent of families belong to next higher range of Rs.20,000 to Rs.40,000. This range comprises of all the non-cultivating families and a few from marginal and small holding groups. The middle range of Rs.40,000-60,000 accounts for 20 per cent of families mainly composed of a third of small farmers, a quarter of medium farmers and some marginal farmers. The next two upper income groups account for a fraction over 50 per cent of the families. Majority of the families falling in these two upper ranges are from medium and large holdings.

However, it may also be noted that there need not

be a positive correlation between the size of holding and range of incomes. Obviously, the component of non-farm incomes, especially from dairying, is quite considerable apart from the intra differences in crop pattern and crop intensities affecting the agricultural incomes irrespective of size of operational holdings. The progress in dairying leads to a more balanced development of the rural economy and improvement in the economic status of poor people associated with livestock.[8]

The importance of dairying for the beneficiary families would be clear when we look at the relative contribution of different sources to total household incomes.

Table 2 shows the pattern of relative proportions of incomes derived from different sources according to the operational land holding groups. The pattern reveals that 92 per cent of families are found in groups that derive greater proportions of incomes from dairying than any other occupation or source. The only exceptional group where income from agriculture is greater than dairying is the large size of holding (above 4 hectares).

The income from dairying is as high as 96 per cent for those who are landless, 75 per cent for those with marginal land holding, 66 per cent in small and 56 per cent in medium size holding. Even in large holdings, income from dairying is 30 per cent of the total income. At the overall sample level, the contribution of dairying to total income is about 60 per cent, followed by agriculture with 36 per cent and other sources about four per cent of the total household incomes.

To assess the impact of the cattle breeding programme, a comparison has been made between beneficiaries and non-beneficiaries (chosen from the same areas as beneficiaries with same parameters, except that they have not been affected by BAIF's Programme). The difference between the economic status of beneficiaries and non-beneficiaries is due to the activities of BAIF. The impact of the cattle production programme aimed at improving the local livestock, has transformed the entire economy of the rural household.

Even though the beneficiaries have the alterative government service centers available, they prefer to take the service of BAIF due to differences in attitude, approach and efficiency from the user's standpoint. In response to some pertinent queries, the opinions expressed by the beneficiaries bring out the contrasting scenario in the style of rendering the comparable services. All given a choice, they always prefer an NGO over that of government outlets dealing with similar services.

The case study intended to be feedback on ground realities, to learn about the motivation (campaign), acceptance by the people, the process of delivery of service, perceivable general impact, opinions on strength and weakness of NGO operation and constraints faced by the people in respect of cattle development by BAIF, was undertaken to test the hypothesis that, given a level play ground, the NGO can deliver goods more speedily and efficiently as compared to indifferent bureaucracy at the ground level. There is a built-in apathy to government outlets as the personnel manning them are not sufficiently motivated.

One of the major conclusions that emerge from this case study is that BAIF's approach and style of functioning is far superior to those of government agencies.

People accept and appreciate the apolitical approaches of well professionalized NGOs to deliver the goods. The government at best can divert fund to NGOs, dovetail many of their schemes with NGOs programmes and even selectively assign the feretories to NGOs so as to create a sense of competitive spirit and provoke the government departments and Panchayati Raj institutions to come our of their slumber.

Our suggestion is that only efficient and non-controversial NGOs with a proven track record must be chosen after a thorough appraisal and screening. This job of selection must be assigned to professional expert bodies, the politicians and bureaucrats must deliberately be kept out of screening, selection and monitoring functions.

Sustainable development has to be viewed as a shared responsibility of the government. NGOs and other institution in the society. Therefore, supportive infraction as well as effective collaboration between the government and NGOs is of utmost importance.

For sustainable rural transformation, problem must be overcome in the relationship between the government and the NGOs. The government has to create a conducive social, economic and political environment, in which development of rural areas can take place through a mix of initiatives. On the political front, 73rd and 74th amendments to the Constitution are viewed as conscious efforts at decentralization but the desired degree of success continues to elude us.

In their role as catalysts of rural economic transformation, NGOs serve as a model for government agencies and others which can be replicated elsewhere too. Therefore, NGOs deserve greater financial and technical support.

In the background of ongoing economic reforms favoring globalization and privatization, the NGO sector must be encouraged to play a greater participatory role in the development of the rural economy. In the new scenario where there is greater transparency in the Indian economy, the foreign funding and other agencies are bound to be encouraged to extend financial and technical help to NGOs.

Since the ultimate responsibility of rural development lies with the government, the initiative has to come from the government to involve the NGOs right from the stage of planning and policy formulation.

REFERENCES

1. Pranab Bardhan (1996): Decentralized development, *Indian Economic Review*, Vol. XXXI, No. 2, pp. 139–156 (A revised version of V.K. Ramaswamy Memorial Lecture Sponsored by the Delhi School of Economics, the Indian Statistical Institute and Institute of Economic Growth).
2. Shikha Jha (2002): Strengthening local Government (Rural Fiscal Decentralization in India), *Economic and Political Weekly*, Vol. XXXVII, No. 26, June 29–July 5, Mumbai.
3. Oommen, M.A. (2001): Planning for decentralized Development, *Frontline*, Vol. 18, Issue 25, Dec. 08–21, Chennai.

4. Misra, Suresh and Dhaka, Rajvir S. (2001): Institutional Mechanism for Participatory Rural Development, *Kurukshetra,* Vol. 49, No. 12, Sept., New Delhi.

5. Ahmad Noman Syed (1997): *Rapid Rural Transformation Through Voluntary Action,* M.D. Publication Pvt. Ltd., New Delhi.

6. Government of India, Ministry of Finance, *Economic Survey 2001-2002,* p. 192, New Delhi.

4

Technology Utilization through Rapid Rural Appraisal

The Indian agriculture is not as rosy as it appears. The land under cultivation is shrinking. The only option left is to enhance the productivity per unit area. The job is challenging and difficult too. Yet it is possible provided the scientists, the extension workers, and the farmers interact, understand, be one of compatible size-neutral, simple and acceptable. There are many reasons for a particular technology or a popular among the same society. However, the reasons thereof are yet to be explored, analysed and put in proper perspective for appropriate remedies. This also helps in identifying a set of constraints and appropriate interventions to either reduce the magnitude of the constraints or totally overcome them. The technique generally used and widely designed and administered to a sample drawn from the population. Information is collected, analyzed, interpreted and suggestions offered.

Rapid Rural Appraisal

Recently, a quick method has come in vogue. It underwent some modifications. This, however, is not a substitute to a survey method but it appropriately supplements and complements the well established survey method. This is known as Rapid Rural Appraisal (RRA). It is defined as a systematic semi-structured activity carried out in the field by a multi-disciplinary team and designed to acquire quickly new information and new hypothesis about the rural life.

According to a multi-disciplinary team of plant breeder, plant physiologist and biochemist (handwritten report on the technology utilization employing RRA technique, 1993), RRA is a successful attempt wherein all the information related to the rural life and field problems could be grasped in the proper prospective. In their opinion farmers become open, flexible, and interactive once the bulky questionnaires are kept aside and free dialogue takes place. RRA appeared to them as faster in terms of depth and communication.

The first author was alone while conducting RRA to explore technology utilization and reasons associated thereof. RRA was a small part in her six-week Field Experience Training at the Central Plantation Crops Research Institute, Kasargode, Kerala.

Methodology

The RRA was conducted for four days. Two days were spent in the adopted village and two days in the non-adopted village. A semi-structured exhaustive guideline was prepared to interact with the key informants.

The term 'adopted village' refers to a village adopted by CPCRI for intensive extension activities (lab-to-land programme). The villages, namely, Madhur (adopted) and kudlu (non-adopted) are located at the distance of 12km and 5km respectively from kasargode district headquarters.

Key informants

A total of 14 key informants, seven each from adopted and non-adopted village representing the village society, was chosen after a thorough discussion with elderly people in the village and extension personnel at the grassroots level. The interactions were held with seven key informants in group. A brief profile of the key informants is given below :

Age	*Adopted*	*Non-Adopted*
Young	2	2
Middle	3	4
Old	2	1
Education		
Primary		2
High School	3	5
Graduate	4	
Progressiveness	Yes	Yes
Participation in extension activities		
Read Etinction Literature	Yes	Yes
Office Bearers	Yes	Yes

The key informants were progressive farmers and participator in group farming approach to technology adoption. The group farming is gaining good amount of recognition in Kerala.

Cropping & soil

The important common crop in both the villages coconut. In addition, areca nut, cashew, banana, paddy, pepper, cocoa, vegetables and bevelling are grown. Soil type in adopted village is delayed in valleys, lateritic loam in plains and slopes and hard literate in the summit. The non-adopted village has more or less plain topography with soil type ranging from sandy to lateritic loamy. The cropping pattern in the adopted village indicates that paddy and areca nut are grown in wetlands and valleys, coconut in plains and slopes, cashew in stops and casuarina in the extreme top of the topography whereas coconut and paddy are the main crops in the nonadopted village.

Technology Generation

Mainly Central Plantation Crops Research Institute with headquarters at Kasargode and the Kerala Agricultural University's regional agricultural research station with headquarters at Pilicode are engage in technology generation. The CPCRI is confined to technology generation in the crops of coconut, areca nut, cocoa, and oil palm. The packages of practices are finalized at KAU after thorough deliberations with the research institutions located in Kerala. But need-based and location-specific technology development is rare. This leaves a lot of future scope for technology generation for these villages. As things stand, the local varieties dominate the agricultural scene in important crops like coconut, areca nut and paddy. It does not, however, mean that the farmers are reluctant to adopt high-yielding varieties (HYVs). Since the HYVs were reported to be susceptible to pests and diseases, farmers try them on small scale and in case these do not come up to their expectations, they discontinue the varieties. The HYVs of arecanut are gaining importance compared to the HYVs of coconut due to continuous market demand. Farmers, however, expressed the view that the has do not come well under adverse conditions. Adverse conditions occur due to five-month dry spell every year. While there was a water-logging problem in the rainy season in the adopted village, there appeared sea water inundation into paddy fields in the non-adopted village. Farmers reported that good taste and adequate yield of strain of the local varieties of paddy were the reasons for continuing with local paddy varieties.

Technologies of inter-cropping, mixed cropping and high density multispecies cropping in coconut and areca nut were found to be more common in the adopted village. However, recommended spacing for plantation crops is not judiciously followed. The high labour cost coupled with scarcity of agricultural labour cost coupled with scarcity of agricultural labour constrained the farmers to skip certain farm operations. Some farmers follow certain practices/operations in alternate years. Group management of operations in paddy and coconut is being followed as a labour-saving mechanism. It is a classical example of finding a solution to the most pressing problem from within the village.

Nutrient Management

Nutrient management is highly unscientific. Though quite a good number of farmers in both the villages apply fertilizers even to the local paddy varieties, farmers were reluctant to apply fertilizers to coconut crop. Coconut being a hardy crop yields at least 10-15 need per annum even under adverse conditions. From discussion it could be inferred that a few farmers follow the recommended doze in proper way and the rest either followed or higher doze of fertilizer applications.

Farmers expressed their ignorance of the impact which the nutrient imbalance can have on crop production. Potash, which is essential and needed in larger quantity for coconut, is often skipped. But the same set of farmers applied the required doze of fertilizers to arecanut for the simple reason that it has good market demand. The indifferent attitude of the farmers to the crops in terms of package of practices needs to be changed.

Problems get aggravated due to poor soil fertility status. Soil acidity and indiscriminate use of land further add to the problems. To quote a specific example, there is difficult in root penetration of coconut planted in hard literate soil. The price hike in fertilizers made the farming community doubtful of remunerative agriculture. Unfortunately, the potential of organic matter like green leaves of natural vegetation in the sloppy areas, animal wastes and wood ash has not been explored and exploited as source of nutrients to reduce dependence on fertilizers.

Proper soil and water management has not been followed. In the adopted village, they is water-logging in the rainy season and water deficiency in summer. Lack of proper drainage causes problem in areca nut. The present practice of bringing new soil from other areas to the cultivated field to raiser the level of basins to form drainage channels cannot be an appropriate remedy. Indeed, banking on this practice would lead to far-reaching consequences. Top soil is heavily eroded and lateritic gaps could be seen exposed in Madhur village.

Irrigation & Plant Protection

Irrigation is inevitable. Continuous dry spell of five months in a year is a testimony to the fact. Acute water deficiency during summer poses a serious threat to the farmers. Groundwater table is low and charging is poor. It was one of the reasons why the farmers could not go in for high-yielding varieties. However, progressive farmers use sprinkler irrigation methods.

Farmer use plant protection measures against Mahali disease (fruit drop) of arecanut. However, this disease was reported to be the major concern of the arecanut growers. It causes yield reduction to the time of 80 percent. Lack of integrated management and proper control measures on the part of the farmers could not keep this alarming problem under check. Stem bleeding of coconut, bunchy top of banana, quick wilt of pepper, rhinocrus beetle in coconut, button, shedding in coconut and spindle bug in arecanut were some of the major pests and diseases. Integrated pest and disease management will have to be followed in both the villages.

Post Harvest

Grading, processing and storage were carried out. Loss of quality of arecanuts in terms of reduction in fats, proteins and sugars have been reported. This occurs due to fungal attack. Husked must are more susceptible to fungal attack, post-harvest knowledge, therefore, becomes and important aspect of modern agriculture. Farmers cannot afford to loose heavily on account of ignorance and improper adoption of post-harvest practices. They need to be educated on these aspects.

Economic Condition

The farmers with less than 50 cents expressed the view that they were not entitled for bank loans for agricultural purposes such as pumpsets and wells. Lack of regulated market coupled with exploitation by middle men jeopardized the sincere efforts put in by the marginal farmers. Five nuts for every 1000 coconut are being charged as commission by middlemen. But in case of arecanut, there is the well established marketing system known as Central Arecanut Marketing and Processing Cooperative (CAMPCO) and Kerala Cooperative Marketing and Processing Committee (KCMPC). Arecanut growers have expressed their concern about the possibility of a high price risk in future. The scientists of CPCRI were also of the same opinion, the arecanut production is increasing year after year and the uses of arecanut at present have been limited to chewing. Alternate uses of arecanut will have to be explored before it jeopardize the economic interest of the farmers.

Technology Dissemination

Technology generation and technology dissemination are two components of the same continuum. Both have to go together. Often it has been seen that they do not go together. In both the villages, the agency involved in technology transfer was the Department of Agriculture. In India, major extension work is being carried out by the State Departments of Agriculture in Kerala, each panchayat has a Krishi Bhavan. This is headed by an Agricultural Officer supported by two or three Agricultural Assistants. These members of staff have close contact with the peasants while the scientists of CPCRI and KAU personnel did not have intensive contacts with the farmers. However, interactions were reported in lab-to-land programme. Farmers felt that the interactions between the scientists and the farmers needed to be intensive and strengthened on a continuing basis. In some parts of the adopted village, Krishi Vigyan Vinimaya Kendra organizes fortnightly meetings of farmers to discuss and impress upon the farmers the efficacies of the technologies.

With further interaction, farmers revealed that they were ready to communicate technological information to other farmers. Interestingly, many farmers started adopting new technologies due to the influence of progressive farmers. In Kerala, the literacy is highest. Therefore, farmers read news papers regularly and also popular extension literature as and when supplied. The page allotted of the farmers. An agricultural graduate farmer in nearby village is sought after by the farmers of both the villages. He provides quality seeds/seedlings on demand. The scientists and extension personnel seek his help to influence and pursue the farming community.

In the light of the above facts, the dissemination mechanism needs to be strengthened with built-in mechanism for continuous improvement

Tapping Indigenous Techniques

The time is fully ripe now for the agricultural scientists to become down-to-earth. The wisdom is not specific to a particular set of people. Wisdom lies with every category of farmers. Following brief account is just indicative of the facts:

i. Farmers spray wafer on cashew inflorescence on cloudy days. This reduces the attack of tea mosquito since this induces change in humidity.
ii. Farmers get powdered groundnut cake dispersed in water as attractant trap for rhinoceros beetle in coconut.
iii. Farmers plant small coconut poles in the fields. The birds rest on these poles and catch the insects and caterpillars. During night hours, owls rest on poles and catch rats/rodents.
iv. Spraying ash on paddy field in the early morning. This acts physical barrier and antifeedant for the posts. This calls for increased interaction between the scientists and technology users on a continuing basis to logically and scientifically synthesize the ITKs for integrating them with improved technologies. Such blending will accelerate the dissemination process thereby facilitating adoption expeditiously. The factors like compatibility, ease, less resources and

available skill will positively influence the judgment of the farmers.

Future Research Needs

Once the problems of the area are known and grasped in proper perspective, research projects can be contemplated. By using RRA technique, the scientists can gather relevant information and then formulate a research project for developing appropriate technologies.

A set of clearly defined aspects have emerged:

i. extension system operating at present is not satisfactory. It needs to be strengthened. Lack of awareness of crucial production factors is an outcome of poor extensions system.

ii. The aim of the applied research is to increase productivity of the area and thereby the economic status of the farmers. This emphasizes the need for scientific nutrient management practices. Recommendations on the basis of nutrient status of soil should be made and demonstrated.

iii. There is a possibility of exploring and exploiting the organic sources such as green leaves of natural vegetation, animal wastes and wood ash to reduce the dependence of farmers on costly inorganic fertilizers.

iv. There is need for advocating proper land use planning.

v. Training is essential in proper water and soil management techniques. Demonstration of these aspects is essential.

vi. The low cost labour–saving technologies are essential to fit in the resource endowments of small and marginal farmers.

The RRA has been quite interesting, thought-provoking and challenging technique for exploring the area chosen, It has built-in scope of adding points of enquiries as we proceed on-the-spot.

Glimpses of Poverty Alleviation Programmes

A flood of light has been thrown in recent years in the shape of economic literature relating to the question of defining and measuring poverty. In such attempts rural development has been thought to be an important tool box for minimizing and mitigating abject poverty, gross inequality in income and wealth, chronic unemployment and underemployment. After independence right from the first five year plan, the Community Development Programmes, the National extension service schemes, the Marginal Farmers and Agricultural labourer Agencies, the Small Farmers development Agencies and various sorts of development financing agencies were constituted with institutional approach. Poverty eradication programmes through rural development schemes have got a considerably significant place in almost all the Five year plans but their content and focal points have been varying from plan to plan. For instance the emphasis shifted from the community development in earlier plans to rural agricultural development later on has a marked line to point out the two distinct phases. It was realized after some time that the benefits accruing from agricultural development only widened the gap of inequality between the agriculturists and the landless poor. It was also felt that the problem of tribal development were quite different from those of agriculturists and the landless labourers in the rural areas. Later on a third phase in the Indian planning process came into being in the shape of package programme for the whole community with special stress on rural inhabitants. The Sixth Plan expressly accorded priority to development of agriculture activities allied to agriculture and rural industries. As a matter of fact poverty eradication was one of the principal objectives of the Sixth Five Year Plan. With this end in view, a quantitative target has been laid down aiming to reduce the proportion of population below the poverty line, from 48.4 per cent in 1979-80 to 30 per cent in 1984.85. Of course the objective behind all this gave birth to Integrated Development Programmes such as Integrated Rural Development Programme, Integrated Tribal Development Programme and Integrated Child Development Programme.

The concept of Integrated Rural Development Programme is a multi-level and multicultural concept. It encompasses agriculture industries, education, healthcare, transport, cottage industries etc. on priority basis in favour of the rural poor like landless labourers artisans, small and marginal farmers as also the scheduled castes and scheduled tribes, the policy for poetry alleviation has high hopes from IRDP and the National Rural Employment Programme (NREP). Under the IRDP community Development block has been accepted as the unit of planning and the District Rural Development Agencies as the chief supervisory body at the district level, The administrators at block levels identify genuine beneficiaries and households actually falling below the poverty line (i.e. income less than

Rs. 3,500 per year). They further sub classify them into three subgroups (i.e. Rs. 1,500 or less; Rs. 1,501-2,500 & Rs. 2,501-3,000). Households identified at the lowest bottom are helped first on the ground of justice. According to Planning Commission on the basis of the Mid-term Appraisal of the Sixth Plan, the percentage of poverty on reckoning come down to 42.5 and the total number of persons below the poverty line to 282 million in 1981–82.

Further a new dimension of the planning scenario was visualised in identification of the major problems of poverty. As a consequence of it, many Programmes clustered around alleviation of poverty through the five year plans. Mention may be made of several programmes in this regard such as Rural works programme, Employment cum production scheme (Food for Work Programme) and Antodaya scheme for uplift of the down trodden.

And yet another trend in the structural framework of planning in the country is marked in the form of the Minimum Needs programme and the 20 point programmes right from the Sixth Plan with considerably marked emphasis in the Seventh Plan. These two Programmes give particular preference to the weaker and vulnerable sections of the society by providing health care, housing, education and nutrition facilities to them (specially the Scheduled Castes and the Scheduled Tribes) as the objectives of both Sixth and Seventh Plan indicated. With the same and in view the Small Farmers Development Agency, the Marginal Farmers and Agricultural Labourer Agency and Drought Prone Area Development Programmes also came in to existence. Really the poverty alleviation programme hovers around creation of employment opportunities.

It consists of Rural Landless Employment Guarantee Programme, National Rural Employment programmed, Food for Work, Minimum Wages Act for agricultural labourers and Skill Development Programme.

Actually speaking all these programmes revolve round the pivotal ground of improvement in the conditions of rural areas mitigating the miseries and helplessness of the agricultural labourers, artisans, small and marginal farmers as also the weaker groups of society in the country.

Even the approach to the Seventh Plan also blindly follows the pattern of further intensification of the aforesaid programmes deposit their weaknesses and worse confounding features. The foregoing accounts no doubt reveal that there is multiplicity of diverse and hetergenous but ad-hoc programmes not suited to the chain of a long term continuous planning process with broadbased objective in a particular direction.

Critical Appraisal of the Programmes: Structural weaknesses in the administrative set up at the district and block level have been pointed out by an evaluation study. Another drawback pointed out by the same study is related to frequent transfers of key officials particularly project Officers (DRDA). The data collected for evaluation study are indicative of the fact that only about 26 per cent of the total sample households were selected in the open Gram Sabha meetings. About 74 per cent of the beneficiaries were selected by Block Development Officers and Village level workers. This undoubtedly unfolds that more deserving households were not selected for assistance. Lack of awareness among the rural beneficiaries about the sundry schemes and time lag between sanction and delivery of benefits assets are also limiting factors in this regard. According to the study group report lacunae in recovery of loans by financial institutions from the beneficiaries were found owing to the fact that returns from the schemes were not adequate and incomes realized by the householders were spent on extraneous purposes such as marriages illness, death and other customary functions.

It has been further found that there are abnormal delays in implementation of the programmes due to bureaucratic machinery bifurcating the essentially urgent administrative execution and financial cost which naturally bring about a vicious circle of reappraisal and reapproval with imbalances. There is only type of rigid budget pattern for the entire state or the country as a whole. This is one of the causes that hinders successful block level planning for the conditions, climate, natural resource endowments and social status differ from area to area.

Unnecessary Staff-oriented schemes: There is much more stress on staffing rather than people's participation and creating and furthering infrastructure for continued development. The long hierarchy of staff keeps the Senior Officers mainly busy in solving and taking care of administrative complications and complexities resulting in bickering, indiscipline, dissension and political push and pull. As we are all aware of the kernel truth that recruitment of staff areas, the personnel or the Staff become unwilling and reluctant to their duly in exaction of the Programmes. Consequently they grumble, resent and do not give their due attention.

Neglect of Village and College Industries: In Block level planning, creation of new employment opportunities in the best interest of the poor through the schemes of Khadi Industry and village and cottage industries have not been accorded the desired seriousness and significant role for which the Khadi Gramodyog Commission have been making untiring endeavours for quite some time. In this field it is essentially imperative on the part of the planners and executive body to exercise rethinking on block level planning as an integral part and parcel of spatial planning.

The problems of bonded labourers: A major defect relating to bonded labourers for achieving to bonded labourers for achieving the goals of poverty alleviating efforts is found in liberating the bonded labourers. Undoubtedly it will be easy to free them from the bondage but it is stupendously difficult to rehabilitate them. If there is lack of continued jobs and opening of new opportunities for employment, they are very likely to be captivated into the former bonded situation which wills surely vitiate the aim of poverty alleviation schemes. This problem demands of a new strategy by the government with new vision and innovative designer legislation.

All pervading corruption: Rampant corruption in purchase of cattle, agricultural implements, machinery and conveyances like rickshaw etc. for loaning by different banks and distribution of subsidies greatly reduce profitability and productivity of poverty eradication schemes. The prevalent corruption in bureaucratic cadres and institutional agencies is one of the major factors stultifying the efforts of developmental process meant for mitigating poverty. According to some study groups the success of IRDP suffers from the indifferent and neglectful attitude of the personnel.

Competitive lending absences: There are at present a lot of overlapping variety of institutional lending agencies in the country catering to the credit needs of the people including the rural poor. There is a net-work of co-operative Banks and state co-operative Banks).

There are a number of State Cooperative land development banks with their branches at the district level. The nationalized banks also have been extending their branches liberally in the rural areas giving preference to vulnerable groups of the country. For quite some time a number of Regional Rural Banks are being established for the some end. The State Governments too occasionally advance Taccavi loans to the mass of people particularly during the periods oi natural calamities. In addition to all this the Khadi and Village Industries Commission, also helps to an extent in financing different activities at the national level. Evidently there appears to exist unhealthy competition amongst the credit agencies for meting credit need in the rural areas at the same district level.

Faulty monitoring and evaluation method: Monitoring and evaluation of poverty alleviation programme has come in for many scathing criticisms. K. Sundaram and Suresh D. Tendulkar hold that expenditure of IRDP is not directly related to and can not have a proportional relationship with the poverty alleviation on several counts.[1] Prof. Raj Krishna also has raised questions about the Methodology of monitoring poverty eradication programmes in the Mid-Term Appraisal of the Sixth Plan because of possibilities of considerable multiple counting of beneficiaries under different schemes.[2] The male bias in intra-family members for distribution of food, clothing and other amenities nullifies the assumption that if a household is enabled to cross the poverty line, it would be deemed as the crossing of the line by all its members. This too goes to an extent in hindering the reckoning of poverty intensity of a household

Some Suggestions: The poverty alleviating programmes are administration oriented and time taking. The administrative cadre now requires rejuvenating incentives, training, change in design, formulation of very struck procedures as also structural and behavioral change to treat the poor with sympathetic attitude. In a nut shell an action programme for bringing about radical reforms in the mechanism of service delivery is so essential in the present context. It is also essential to involve the village assemblies for selection of only deserving beneficiary households for assistance under IRDP on the pattern of recommendation made by the study report of the planning commission. The animal husbandry schemes should be launched only in areas where basic infrastructure facilities including marketing support are available.

Financial Assistance: The Central Government should allot sizeable funds for all blocks to the states and the states in turn to the districts and the districts to the blocks in time quite in tune with the schemes/ programmes for development of the people particularly in rural areas. It is suggested that bold steps must be taken hence onward to fortify, strengthen and streamline the monitoring arrangement at the state district and block levels on emulative guidelines of Gujarat and Rajasthan States. Many economists feel that there is urgent necessity for a massive transfer of resources to rural development in view of the multi-sectoral approach and the increasing need of the adoption of new but appropriate technology for creating broach-based employment opportunities to mitigate the pitiable miseries of the poor in rural areas. But the implementation of the schemes should be made by honest and stringent agencies failing which the agencies and officials must be taken to task.

Stabilisation of Population: The benefits of growth process, as experience show in Indian context, gets not only diluted but sometimes extinct because the growth rate of the population is higher than the growth rate of developmental programmes. In view of the explosive growth rate in population in the country, it is quite necessary to include stabilization of population in the block level planning itself on priority basis. But I confidently feel like some other thinkers that the simple method based on voluntary wishes and persuasive incentives for making the family planning scheme a success will not go a long in solving the knotty problem of population control.

Need for motivated team of the personnel: Majority of the economists are unanimous on the point that unless and until development schemes are promoted by a motivated team of the functionaries with high morale and dedication with a keen sense of leadership, the real-interest of the poor in our country will not be served in spite of the best intention and pious hopes of the Government and the programmes stands in need of detailed information about the target groups, household size, intrahousehold distribution of expenditure on consumption, degree of leakage of benefits transferred on the real testimony and assessment of poverty. There is no doubt, in absence of such minute details, programme evaluation would remain a superficial paper exercise resulting in huge wastage of valuably constrained resources in the country.

Revamping Hazardous approach to the planning: The foregoing analysis and scanning of the various poverty alleviation programmes shows that only a peacemeal approach to the whole problem of roach to the whole problem of poverty alleviation policy has been made. Several programmes and schemes have been launched through the five year plans at different stages and at different times. But in course of time, each of these schemes found itself relegated to the background in favor of something new with preferential treatment confounding and disappointing the people. The huge wastage emerging from such programmes has been highlighted by sundry studies conducted on the functioning of IRDP. Really this problem should grip the serious attention of the planners for rethinking with the objective of correcting the hap hazardous approach to the planning. It is night-time for the implementers of the programmes to avoid duplication, wastage and worse confusion in getting funds from the different credit agencies and ministries with unhealthy competition going on. It has become now more essential to coordinate the diverse and conflicting programmes at the block level for achieving the goal of the scheme. It is also suggested that the workers at the village level must belong to the block in its vicinity and not to any ministry hailing from outside distant places. There is the dire necessity that the different lending agencies are integrated and interwoven on the model of Hazari Committee report recommending integration of primary village cooperatives and primary land development banks in a phased manner so that all categories of farmers can get short, medium and long term loans according to their needs from the same lending level agency. The role of National Bank for Agriculture and Rural Development (NABARD) to regulate disbursement of rural credit by the cooperatives, the commercial banks and Regional Rural Banks is, beyond doubt, most appreciable and commendable but the consolidated achievement stemming there-from is yet to be realized. There is still much to be done.

To conclude, the Seventh Plan must implement such programmes effectively and stringently despite their ad-hocism in nature failing which the poor would be forced to a more degrading position and hopeless exploitation. I am afraid in future such poverty alleviation programmes may give rise to upheaval and revolt pervading political, economic and social life of the whole country if a serious thought is not given to the implementing machinery of the programmes.

The states which are identified as socially advanced states have lower CBR and also lower CDR, than the national average of CBR and CDR. This is also true for the states which are economically advanced. The correlation co-efficient shows an inverse relation between the levels of economic development and levels of mortality and fertility and also between the levels of social development and levels of mortality and fertility.

Thus, the socio-economic development in the states of India is responsible for bringing demographic changes by the decline of birth rate and death rate. It may be also possible to perceive that the social development has more contribution towards the demographic changes as observed from the value of correlation co-efficient. The economic development alone can bring about the demographic change through social development and vice-versa. However, there could be a time-log between these two types of development. At least, there are two states in India have illustrated such situation. One is Kerala, where the economic development is initiated through the social development. The reverse may be true for Punjab where social development led by economic development. Otherwise, both social and economic development are in operation simultaneously in most of the Indian states. The states are Maharashtra, Tamil Nadu, Gujarat, Karnataka, West Bengal, Haryana and Andhra Pradesh.

REFERENCES

1. ON EVALUATING POVERTY Eradication programme. Dr. H.J. Sharma.
2. Documents & Drafts of all the five year plans (including the Seventh Five Year Plan) *Yojana,* Vol, 29 No 18 October 1-15-1985 page 28. Op. Cit., p. 15.

5

Lead Bank Approach

The economic and commercial progress of any region is crucially influenced by the effective performance of its banking sector. In a developing country like India, the role of the banking sector becomes particularly invisible.

The banking sector has to perform a number of promotional and corrective functions. Desirable economic and commercial achievements are possible only if the banking sector grows in a balanced manner and responds readily to the calls of the system. Many innovative experiments are necessary to have balanced growth of the banking sector. By "balanced growth" we mean that the several parts or regions or areas of the economy will have simultaneous growth opportunities in terms of physical amenities and financial allocations. All elements of imbalance and imperfections will automatically be eliminated.

There was much thinking and talking about the salient features of "social control" of banks in early sixties in India. Social control of commercial banks was tried to some extent. Social ownership and control of the banking institutions were expected to do the spade work for a new economic order then. But the remark by the late dynamic Prime Minister, Mrs. Indira Gandhi is one of the public speeches in 1968 "social control is just half way to socialism and it doesn't attack the foundations of concentration of economic power." So more objectives oriented programmes were complemented subsequently. Nationalization becomes the natural answer in this direction of 'dynamic reshaping of values and functions[1].

The Banking Commission (1969) headed by Mr. Sariya encouraged the nationalization of commercial banks in July 1969. The socio-economic objectives and reforms of nationalization have been encouraged. The Reserve Bank of India began to make a number of enquiries about further possible changes in the banking sectors. The Nariman Committee on Banking Development and the Gadgil Study Group considered the logic of the bank scheme and recommended the introduction of that in 1969. As a result, the Annual Action Plan scheme was born towards the end of 1969. This pragmatic scheme is considered to economically inspiring and historically significant.[2]

A committee of bankers headed by Mr. F.K.F. Nariman was set up by the Reserve Bank of India in 1969 after the historical nationalization of fourteen commercial banks. It studied the problem of imbalances in the banking sectord and submitted by its findings quickly. A study group of the National Credit Council worth Prof. Dr. Gadgil as its chairman also scrutinized the same problem parallelly and presented its views. Both the Committee and the Group recommended the introduction of the Annual Action Plan Scheme. The standing committee of Bankers endorsed the Annual

Action Plan Scheme in December 1969. The RBI accepted the recommendations of the Nariman Committee and the Gadgil Study Group and hence the "Area approach" to banking came into being in India Banking structure. The Annual Action Plan Scheme was introduced towards the year end of 1969 in India.[3]

The introduction of the Annual Action Plan Scheme was considered to be a major leap forward and significant phase in the progress of development banking in India. The Annual Action Plan Scheme gives importance to locate of bank branches and their operational efficiency. A revenue district is kept as a unit of operation. Each district will have a "Annual Action Plan" usually a commercial bank will play the "Lead role" in the comprehensive development of the district concerned.[4]

Statement of the Problem

This study has taken into account the embarking of the Annual Action Plan scheme in Tiruchirapalli District, Tamil Nadu. This Tiruchirappalli district is centrally located in the state of Tamilnadu. Tiruchirappalli is one of the well developed district in the state. The east while attempt was to find out the overall activities of Annual Action Plan in this district.

In this district Indian Overseas Bank has assigned to "Annual Action Plan" which can render remarkable services to the developmental activities. It includes the implementation schemes in various blocks among sectoral wise, scheme-wise and even region-wise allocation.

Recently this bank has conducted effectively implementing the poverty eradication programme in a successful manner. In general this study is an overall synoptic view of the working of the Annual Action Plan scheme in this district.

Importance of the Study

Under the Annual Action Plan scheme, as a case in point, Indian overseas Bank allotted in Tiruchirapalli district and was asked to play the primary role. It has been expect to act as a leader to bring about a coordination of different banking institutions. To the interest of district development. The RBI also spelt out functions of the Annual Action Plan. This scheme has been in operation for more than fifteen years.

However, it is also felt that the Annual Action Plan has served its purpose only in certain "Selected Spheres." It is also alleged that certain vital functions expected to be performed by the Annual Action Plan is being neglected. In this light of certain criticism, a review of operations of the "scheme" is necessary for such a review would throw light on the reasons for the neglect of certain functions and to take necessary steps to overcome the problems in the implementation of the Annual Action Plan scheme in the proper perspective.

Aspects and Facts

In analysing the pattern of operation of the Annual Action Plan Scheme in Tiruchirapalli District between 1995 and 2000 the following functional and structural aspects and facets are taken into consideration:

a) Resume of resources potential and ability of the Annual Action Plan to bear the responsibility.

b) Availability of other banking institutions.

c) Availability of developmental agencies.

d) Impressionistic surveys and credit plans.

e) Bank Branch expansion efforts with a rural slant.

f) Role of Regional Rural Bank-Pandyan Grama Bank

g) Village Adoption scheme.

h) Pattern of lending

i) Indian Overseas Bank's capability to play the roles of a liaison agent and a coordinator.

j) Positive changes effected in the economic and commercial conditions between 1979 and 1982.

k) Structural changes effected to rectify organisational imbalances.

l) Methods adopted to facilitate prompt and easy repayments or revenue recovery methods.

m) Post-credit follow up actions.

n) Acquiring intimate knowledge of place, positions and problems.

o) Encouragement to self-employment schemes.

p) Employment generation efforts.

q) Provision of inspiring leadership to individuals and institutions or cooperation from institutions and the public in general. Under the LSB both corrective and promotive measures have been adopted in a rigorous way.

Objectives of the Study

The present research work aims to study the working of the Annual Action Plan scheme in Trichirapalli District in 1999-2000 to 2003-2004. It makes a special case study of the working of Annual Action Plan i.e., Indian Overseas Bank. In this district Indian Overseas Bank is working as the Annual Action Plan with their branches of 104 scattered throughout the district both in the urban areas and rural areas. This bank has extended financial assistance to agriculture, industry and tertiary and services sectors. It also implemented more schemes on the basis of bank wise block wise and sectoral wise classification of loans. Evaluation of the working of the Annual Action Plan scheme has a special significance as it constitutes a study in mass banking. If the Annual Action Plan is performing in the right direction it means poorer sections are benefited more and the unbanked far flung rural areas are having better opportunities to develop. In other words, in order to study of working of Annual Action Plan scheme is very important as well as noteworthy.

Objectives

1) To study the general working procedure of the Annual Action Plan scheme in the district.
2) To analyse the method of disbursing loans on various schemes among different taluks in this District.
3) To narrate the type of schemes undertaken by the Annual Action Plan and the total number of beneficiaries.
4) To analyse the total allocations and its actual

achievements of banks on various sectors viz., priority sector, Industry tertiary sector etc.

5) To review the financial performance of the bank especially its disbursal and the recovery of loans.

Methodology

Hypotheses

The following hypotheses have been formulated by the researcher

1. There is no uniformity in the distribution of loans to various sectors.
2. Distribution of loans among different blocks in the district is not the same.
3. Agriculture and other allied activities have received the highest percentage in the total allocation.
4. There is a significant difference in branch expansion before and after introduction of Annual Action Plan scheme.

Limitations of the Study

Essentially, the study was exploratory in nature. Hence it combined primary and secondary sources of data to verify the objectives indicated. Data were gathered through multichannels and various sources. Further, the scarce resources at the disposal of the researcher limited the scope of this investigation. The methodology followed and tools employed in the analysis of the data also stand on an experimental plane. These involve certain merits as well as demerits of their own and also reflect the limitations of the data base of the Banks in Tiruchirapalli District. Due to time constraint the researcher was not able to touch all the broad fields of its functions. This is a serious lacunae.

REFERENCES

1. D.M. Mithani, *An Anatomy of Indian Banking,* Deep & Deep Publishers, Second Edition, New Delhi 1995, P. No. 96.
2. Report of the Reserve Bank of India, 1970.
3. Oscar Lange, *Socialism and Planning,* Himalaya Publishing House, New Delhi, 1952, p. 69. Banking Commission Report, 1969, p. 5. Government of India.
4. *Ibid.*

6

Area Profile and Methodology

Location

Tiruchirapalli district forms the nucleus of the state of Tamil Nadu, without any sea cost. It lies between 10.35^0 and 11.30^0 of the northern Latitude and between 77.30^0 and 79.30^0 of Eastern Longitude. It is bounded by Salem and South Arcot districts in the North, Thanjavur district in the east, Pudukottai, Madurai and Pasumpon Muthuramalingam district in the south and by Anna and Periyar district in the west.

The district is located above the mean sea level of 83 meters. But for the short range of pachamalai hills in the north, the Rangamalai in the extreme south of Karur Taluk. The Vallimalai in the southern part of Kulithalai Taluk. Malai kovil Earumpeeswarar in the east part of Trichy Taluk.

The Tiruchirappalli district is practically having plain terrain.

From the days of Chola kings Tiruchirappalli is a important place in the political life of the south.

Rainfall

The year has been divided into four seasons and the details of the rainfall, received are presented Table 1.

Table 1

Seasonwise Distribution of Normal Rainfall in Tiruchirapalli

S.No.	*Name of the duration of the Seasons*	*Normal Rainfall*	*Percentage of Total*
1.	South west monsoon June to September	274.30	32.43
2	North East Monsoon October to December	394.80	46.85
3	Winter period January to February	40.50	4.81
4	Hot Weather Period March to May	134.00	15.91
	Annual Normal Rainfall	842.60	100.00

Source: District Statistical Office, 2004.

The district receives the heaviest rainfall during the North East monsoon followed by south West monsoon.

Land Use Pattern

The district is spread over a geographical area of 11.12 lakhs heat area. The net area shown in 52.40 percentage of the geographical areas.

Distribution of Holdings

The details of the distribution of land holdings are given in Table 2.

Table 2

Size of Land Holding in Tiruchirapalli District

S. No.	Size of Land Holding	Number	Percentage Total
1.	Marginal (Below 1 ha*)	2,31,014	50.25
2.	Small (3-2 ha)	1,22,931	26.74
3.	Medium (3-4 ha)	69,290	15.07
4.	Large (above 4 ha)	36,486	7.94

*1 HECTARE = 22472 ACRES

Source : Statistical Office, Trichy 2004.

Table 3

Land Use Pattern in Tiruchirapalli District

S.No.	Particulars	Area in hectare	Percentage of Total Area
1	Forest	33,542	3.22
2	Barren uncultivable land	40,529	4.65
3	Land but non-agricultural use	1,45,913	14.12
4	Cultivable waste lands	40,694	4.04
5	Pasture and grazing	45,530	4.61
6	Orchards, the crop's and groves	12,590	1.13
7	Current follows	1,33,501	12.00
8	Other follows	32,301	2.91
9	Net Area Shown	5,33,090	52.43
	Total	10,62,123	102.10

Source: Statistical Office, Trichy, 2004.

As seen in the table the marginal farmers form the major chance the total number of land holding.

The average size of the operational holding for the district is 1.32 hectares.

Industrial Units

There are about 37 large scale industrial units, 3725 small scale Industrial Units and tiny sectors sheds in Tiruchirapalli.

Among the large scale units, BHEL at Tiruverumbur, Small Arms Factory at Thuvakudi, Dalmia Cement Factory at Dalmiaouram, Chetti Nadu Cements at Puliyur, Sugar Factories at Pettavaithalai, Pugalur and Kattur. Tamil Nadu News Prints Ltd. – Pugalur and Paper Limited in Karur taluk are worth mentioning.

Small Scale Industries

SSI Units are found in the manufacturing of machine tool parts, metal products, paper products, mineral products, textile products, chemical products, rubber products, plastic products, petroleum products, and wooden reproduces.

The most important cottage and village industries are handloom, mat weaving, basket making, pottery, brick blacksmithy, carpentry, leather tanning, footwear and artificial gem processing.

There are also grocery shops, ten stalls, petty shops, sundries, fruits and vegetable stalls, cycle lending shops, tailoring shops, medical shops and cloth shops.

Population

The total population of the District was 36,06,033 out of this population 74.88 per cent (i.e. 26,64,214) the rural population.

Occupation

Occupation determines the sources of income from which living standards are identified. The details of occupational distribution are given below:

Table 4

Occupational Distribution of Population in Tiruchirapalli District

S.No.	*Name of occupation*	*Population*		
		Total	*Rural*	*Percentage to Total*
1	Main Workers	14,75,262	11,90,923	80.73
2	Cultivators	5,76,703	5,59,665	97.05
3	Agricultural Labourers	4,61,221	4,43,384	94.18
4	House and industry, Manufacturing, processing, servicing and repair	62,001	43,019	69.38
5	Other workers	3,75,338	1,53,955	41.02

Source : District Statistical Office, Trichy, 2001.

Out of the total workers 80.73 per cent are rural workers and 97.05 per cent of the workers are cultivators and agricultural labourers.

Literacy

The data pertaining to literacy in Tiruchirapalli district in Tamilnadu is given in Table 5.

Table 5: The Literacy Rate in Tiruchirapalli District

S.No.	*Particulars*	*Literate Population*	*Literacy rate*
1	No. of Literate persons	16,47,804	45.6
2	No. of Rural Literate persons	10,13,981	38.0
3	No. of Urban Literate persons	6,33,823	67.2
4	No. of Literate Male	10,63,290	58.4
5	No. of Rural Literate Male	6,96,290	52.1
6	No. of Urban Literate Male	3,66,783	76.1
7	No. of Literate Female	5, 84,514	32.6
8	No. of Rural Literate Female	3,17,474	24.9
9	No. of Urban Literate Female	2,67,040	57.8

Source: Primary data.

Banking Facilities

Tiruchirapalli district has a closely network of bank branches. There are 316 branches of Commercial Banks functioning, of which 217 are rural branches while 33 branches are in semi-urban centres and 66 branches are in urban centres. 956 villages in the district have been allotted to 217 branches under service.

Table 6

Bank Branch Network

	No. of Banks	*No. of Branches*
State Bank Group	3	47
Nationalised commercial Banks	18	196
Private Sector Banks	13	73
Total	34	316

Source : Primary Data.

The action plan prepared by the DIC has been dovetailed with the Annual Action plan 1988 prepared by the Annual Action Plan to ensure credit assistance from financial institutions and achieve the goal of industrial development in the district.

District Banking Statistics

Average population served per branch in Tiruchirapalli district	11,784
National Average Achieved	15,500
National Average Aimed	17,000
Number of banked block Head Quarters	32
(All block Head Quarters have bank branches)	
Percentage of rural branches to the total number of branches in the district	50
Number of specialized branches	9

List of Bank Branches in Tiruchirapalli District at on 1.4.2004

S.No.	*Name of the Bank*	*Number of Branches*			
		Urban	*Semi-urban*	*Rural*	*Total*
1	State Bank of India	7	13	23	43
2	State Bank of Mysore	1	—	—	1
3	State Bank of Travancore	1	2	—	3
	Sub -Total	9	15	23	47
4	Allahabad	—	1	—	1
5	Andhra Bank	1	—	—	1
6	Bank of Baroda	1	2	4	7
7	Bank of Maharashtra	1	—	—	1

8	Bank of India	2	2	12	16
9	Canara Bank	4	5	18	27
10	Central Bank of India	2	2	2	6
11	Corporation Bank	1	—	—	1
12	Dena Bank	1	—	—	1
13	Indian Bank	13	13	14	40
14	Indian Overseas Bank	5	11	49	65
15	New Bank of India	1	—	—	1
16	Punjab National Bank	2	2	4	8
17	Punjab & Sind Bank	1	—	—	1
18	Syndicate Bank	1	2	2	5
19	Union Bank of India	1	2	6	9
20	UCO Bank	2	1	2	5
21	Vijaya Bank	1	—	—	1
Sub – Total		**49**	**58**	**126**	**243**
22	Bank of Madura Ltd.	6	2	6	14
23	Bharat Overseas Bank Ltd.	1	—	2	3
24	Catholic Syrian Bank Ltd.	1	1	1	3
25	Dhanalakshmi Bank Ltd.	1	—	—	1
26	Federal Bank Ltd.	1	—	—	1
27	The Karnataka Bank Ltd.	1	—	—	1
28	The Karur Vysya Bank Ltd.	2	5	4	11
29	City Union Bank Ltd.	1	3	3	7
30	Lakshmi Vilas Bank Ltd.	3	7	10	20
31	Nedungadi Bank Ltd.	1	—	—	1
32	The South Indian Bank Ltd.	1	—	6	7
33	Tamil Nadu Mercantile Bank Ltd.	1	1	—	2
34	Vysya Bank Ltd.	1	—	1	2
	Sub total	**21**	**19**	**33**	**73**
Commercial Banks – Total		**70**	**77**	**159**	**316**
35	District Central Co-op Bank Ltd.	7	20	14	41

36	TNSC Land Dev. Bank Ltd.	1	10	—	11
37	Trichy City Co-op. Bank Ltd.	5	—	—	5
	Sub - Total	13	30	14	57
38	State Financial Institution	1	—	—	1
	Grand Total	**84**	**106**	**184**	**374**

Methodology

The researcher has prepared a separate questionnaire which contains essential questions required for her study purpose. Questions like type of loans sanctioned, amount of recovery, allocation of loan amount to various sectors viz., Priority Sector, Industrial Sector, SSI sector, Teritary Sector and other schemewise loans etc. It also deals the information about the amount of recovery and the review of the implementation of the schemes etc.

Data Collection

This research is built up by both the primary data and secondary data. Data has been obtained from Regional Manager's Office - Indian Overseas Bank, Trichy and other Block Development Offices etc. Secondary data - i.e. the records of Indian Overseas Bank Annual Action Plan, Annual Credit Plan, Schemewise/Sectorwise/Blockwise performance of loans obtained from various branches are gathered from their Annual Financial records.

Statistical Tools

The study is explorative in nature. So the researcher is entirely relied upon the 'Case Study Method'

Eventhough the possibility of selection of sample is possible, but for time constraint, the researcher has specifically preferred for 'Random Sample Method'. By this technique, 5 banks are selected at random.

Period of the Study

The present research deals only for a short span of time i.e., 4 years only i.e., from March 1999-2000 to 2002-2003. About six months time period has been spared by the researchers for collecting the required data.

7

Review of Literature

In this Chapter, research studies conducted by various researchers, in various parts of India, on the working and impact of the Annual Action Plan Scheme, is dealt with. For, such a review of literature is not only meaningful but also relevant for any researcher. Accordingly, the secondary information collected from various journals and survey reports is put forth, on the Annual Action Plan Scheme. According to Paul V. Young, review of literature enables a researcher either to support the hypothesis formulated or to interpret a different conclusion, owing to certain basic structural conditions. Thus a comparative study puts things in their right respective, notwithstanding the limitations.[1]

1. Studies related to Annual Action Plan's Area Development.

2. Studies that examine the performance of Annual Action Plans in many sectors.

According to Morris R. Cohen & Ernest Nagel "Review of Literature sheds light on the various aspects of the particular theme, chosen by a researcher and it provides the necessary background for drawing supporting evidence in favour of a particular argument."[2]

Goode and Hatt[3] observe in their Methods in Social Research, the significance of review of literature as under: "Review of Literature is a compendium of related materials that have been already published on a particular area of research that will be useful for selecting or discarding information related to a particular topic."[3]

A. Raman, Meenakshi and Thiyagarajan in their report on the credit planning cell stated "the area approach to the rural lending's has a number of advantages like the ease and convenience in identification credit follow up and recovery better service to the borrowers at lower cost, facility to serve a large number of accounts per bank staff, greater opportunities for acquiring intimate knowledge of the are and people and better scope for establishing liaison with the Government officials and other development agencies.[4]

"The working of the Annual Action Plan Scheme in Maharastra and Gujarat, was reviewed by the two study groups constituted by the R.B.I. in 1975. The combined report for the two states has stressed the importance of collective action by the banks and other agencies for district development and made a number of recommendations to improve the working of the Annual Action Plan Scheme.[5]

Prof. R.P. Goel " ...More than one bank may be asked to play the lead role in a certain area considering its special requirements. Along with the public Sector banks, the private sector banks will also be provided with the opportunity to play the lead role, if they enjoy the capability and inclination. A Annual Action Plan in this district shall not enjoy monopoly powers in banking business of the area."

Annual Action Plans are expected to open new branches in the unbanked areas and concentrate in the direction of helping financially the weaker sections in terms of making advances and extending loan facilities and providing business proposals, and strategies for promotion in commercial ventures in consultation with the other partners in progress.[6]

Filling in the credit gaps of the areas in an effective manner will be given top priority in the functional pattern of the Annual Action Plans. Credit gaps of various types will be systematically eradicated. The Annual Action Plans act as coordinating agencies and thus integrate the functions of different institutions and departments. They act as a consortium leaders.[7]

All the districts excluding the metropolitan cities were allotted to different banks. Each of these banks was expected to play a lead role or as a consortium of banks and other financial institutions of its area in promoting the development scheme in co-ordination with various agencies of central and state Governments.[8]

Under the Annual Action Plan Scheme all the district in the country have been allotted among public sector banks and a few private sector banks. Each commercial bank is expected to survey the potential for banking development in the allotted districts to identify institutional and credit gaps to take the initiative in endeavouring to fill them and thus intensively involve itself in the process of economic advancement of the district concerned, in sum the promotion of the district through the medium of banks.[9]

Any particular commercial bank in a district can perform the functions, like covering all unbanked or rural area, covering all the sections of the economy and to act a lead role which will creates a favourable banking climate and accelerate the process of growth.[10]

Santhakumari[11], Rajendran[12], and Rajmohan[13] encouraged "... The close involvement of the Annual Action Plan with a particular area will not only result in deposit mobilisation, but also in the expansion of finance to agriculture and small industries, individual banks would make a detailed survey of their operation and the potential in that area for economic growth and evolve schemes to accelerate their involvement in their respective areas.

Under the Annual Action Plan Scheme intensive and thorough studies of the credit needs and development potentialities of the district will be made suitable and suitable credit plans shall be prepared. The Annual Action Plan Scheme also makes critical assessment of the past economic activities of the district and suggests methods of correction in a correlating manner".[13]

The main idea of Annual Action Plan Scheme is the preparation of annual credit plan. A credit plan is a logical assessment of the resources available in an area with the possible avenues of economic advancement. It is a comprehensive records of the various activities and sections of an area. It will guide future economic efforts. The Annual Action Plan Shall play the role of a friend, philosopher and guide to people in the wider spectrum.

Under the "service Area Approach", areas are identified and then allotted to each rural and semi urban branch for financial support and the fulfillment of their credit needs. Each branch has a coverage of 15 to 25 villages under its operational areas which is technically known as service area for the purpose of credit and banking services.[14]

The Annual Action Plan must undertake the depth studies of area would be blue prints of action for the various agencies for the development of that area within a period of say 5 years and should clearly delineate not only the banking activities in that area but the role of commercial banks in effectively translating the blue print into reality.

Working of Annual Action Plans

The Annual Action Plan Scheme provides a new strategy of banking and areas development in the branch expansion programme of banks in the post-nationalization phase of banking growth in the country.

The idea of Annual Action Plan scheme was initiated by the Gadgil study group of the National Credit Council in October 1969. Realizing the deficiency of banking facilities in the rural sector, the Gadgil study Group recommended the adoption of an area approach to evolve plans and programmes for the development of an adequate banking and credit structure in the rural areas. This idea was further endorsed by the Nariman Committee (The Committee of Bankers on Branch Expansion Programmes of Public Sector Banks) in its report submitted in November, 1969. The Committee recommended that each public sector bank should act as a "Annual Action Plan" by concentration on certain districts to fulfil its social obligations.

Following the recommendations of these two committees, the reserve Bank of Indian introduce the "Annual Action Plan Scheme" towards the end of 1969. Under the scheme, 398 districts in the country were allotted to the public sector banks and a few private sector banks. They were supposed to play the role of leaders in banking development.

The Annual Action Plan Scheme did not imply monopoly of the Annual Action Plan in banking business in the district. It only conferred leadership. The Annual Action Plan was to act as a consortium leader for coordinating the activities of all credit institutions cooperative banks, commercial banks and others-in its allotted districts for expansion of branch banking facilities and catering to the needs of rural areas. In short, the Annual Action Plans are assumed to play the role of 'catalytic agents' of banking and rural economic development in their respective lead districts. In short, "each bank is a leader, coordinator and a guide in the district allotted to it."

Functions of Annual Action Plan

The following are the major functions of a Annual Action Plan:-

1. To survey the resources and potential for banking development by identifying unbanked centers in the allotted districts.
2. To set up branches in a phased manner.
3. To identify and study local problems.

4. To find out the number of industrial and commercial units and other establishments which do not have banking accounts or depend mainly on moneylenders.
5. To evolve an integrated credit plan by examining the shortage of marketing facilities for agricultural produce and industrial output, stocking of fertilizers and other agricultural inputs and other services catering to local needs.
6. To recruit and train banking staff for counselling the small borrowers and farmers in the priority sectors and follow-up and inspection of the end-use of bank credit.
7. To provide assistance to other primary lending agencies, and
8. To keep contacts and liaison regularly with government and semi-government agencies.

The Annual Action Plans, as such, are required to chalk out and implement "area planning". They have to integrate their Annual Action Plan schemes with district plans for an effective distribution of credit, along with expanded banking facilities as per local needs.

Working and Progress of the Annual Action Plan Scheme

The Reserve Bank of India had advised the Annual Action Plans to prepare District Credit Plans for their lead districts and implement them. By July 1978, with the preparation of credit plans was completed.

However, due to lack of uniformity in these plans, the Annual Action Plans were advised to terminate them by December 1979 and to prepare new credit plans for the period 1980-82 as per the guidelines suggested by the Reserve Bank. The Reserve Bank stressed the following objectives of bank lending in its guidelines:-

1. To finance labour–intensive schemes which generate employment;
2. To assist weaker sections in all possible ways to improve their productivity;
3. To help increase productivity of land and other allied sectors which would reduce unemployment and improve their income standards.

It has also suggested that the District Credit Plans must be aligned with credit-based development schemes. Further, they should be prepared on a blockwise basis. A District Credit Plan should be accompanied by a separate action-oriented annual plan.

A greater degree of uniformity is seen in the presentation of District Credit Planes and Annual Action Plans in the second and the third rounds during 1980-82 and 1983-85 respectively.

The third round of DCP ended in March 1985. However, the Reserve Bank of India was to provide new guidelines in view of the Seventh Five Year Plan for the fourth round of DCPs. But till October 1986, these could not be finalized. So the Reserve Bank advised the Annual Action Plans to prepare their Annual Action Plans for 1987 broadly on the basis of its earlier guidelines.

However, the new guidelines for the preparation of the fourth round of DCPs for the period January

1988 to December 1990 have been finalized and approved by the High communicated to all Annual Action Plans in March, 1987.

Action Plans

In September 1985, the public sector banks chalked out their Action plans for the period November 1985 to December 1987.

The Action plans involve several measures for improvement in the quality of service and operational efficiency of the banks. These include:-

1. Steps towards revamping credit management and improving the quality of loan assets.
2. Classification of advances on the basis of health codes, timely renewal and review of credit limits.
3. Enforcing operational and monitoring mechanisms to check overdues.
4. Imposing financial discipline on the borrowers.
5. Improvements in the payments mechanism.
6. Prompt balancing of books of accounts.
7. Quicker submission of returns.
8. Inter-bank reconciliation.
9. Improvement of customer services in banks.
10. Improvement in-house keeping.

There have been quarterly reviews of the progress of the Action Plans with a view to help the bank managements as well as the reserve bank to assess the performance of banks.

The Action Plans have been successful in improving

in-house keeping, customer services and also profitability of banks. But their performance with regard to overdues has, however, remained unsatisfactory, as the overdues accounted for 20 per cent of bank lending to priority sectors and 11.5 per cent of lendings to the non-priority sectors at end December 1986.

REFERENCES

1. P.V. Young, *Research Methodology and Scientific Methods*.
2. Morris R. Cohen & Ernest Nagel, *An Introduction to Logic and Scientific Methods*, p. 3.
3. Goode & Hatt, *Methods in Social Research*, Tata McGraw Hill Inc., New Delhi, 1986, p. 5.
4. A. Raman, Meenakshi & Thiagarajan, "Report of the credit planning cell", 1978, p. 7.
5. Report of the study group on the working of Annual Action Plan scheme in Gujrarat and Maharastra, RBI, Bombay, Dec. 1972.
6. Myint H.: "The Economics of the Developing Countries", 1965.
7. Rao V.L. "Progress of Development Banking Commission", 1969.
8. Varshneya, J.S., "Bank Nationalisation and after", *Yojana*, Vol.30, No. 13, July 16 to 31, 1986, p. 6.
9. L.D'Mello "Annual Action Plan Scheme and Role of Rural Banks", *State Bank of India Monthly Review*, Feb. 1976, P. 68.
10. K. Chandrasekar, "Special Distribution of commercial Banking", *Southern Economist*, Vol. xxxi, No. 13, Sep. 15, 1986, p. 9.

11. Santhakumari, "A study of the working of the regional rural banks in India", 1988, p. 116.

12. Rajendran, *Working of Lead Bank Scheme in Trichy District*, 1987, p. 32.

13. Rajmohan, *Lead Bank Scheme a synoptic view*, 1999, p. 27.

14. A.M. Banarjee, " Service Area Approach" – Lead Bank Scheme in Sangli District, Maharashtra, *Kurukshetra*, volume XXXI, No. 26, 1999, p. 29.

8

Analysis and Discussion

In the preceding chapter researcher has so for dealt the principles and procedures involved under the Annual Action Plan Scheme.

Now an attempt has been made to identify the factors responsible for and an allocation to various sector on the basis to its priority sector or any other factors.

A detailed analysis is made about its fixation of targets and its actual achievements achieved by the I.O.B. in Trichy District. It also deals with the review of the demand and recovery position of the bank during the study years.

During the year 1990-1997 the total financial assistance allocated to the agriculture and other allied agricultural sectors was estimated as Rs. 6,461. 87 lakhs, Rs. 1,749.13 to the industries sector and Rs.1,831.78 crores to the services sector. Regarding the achievement made by the bank on various sectors have been estimated as 94,624 persons on the agricultural sector 1,654 in the industrial sector and 10,102 in the services sector.

The overall performance of these schemes benefited to 21380 persons. Among the total target of 94777. So a percentage of achievement was only in meagre (26%).

To depict the sectoral distribution of loans under the Service Area Approach in the year 1988 major sectors like agriculture, Industry, services and other sectors, lane received greater attention in the minds of the banking researcherities. It briefly summarizes the actual allotment to the various sectors is show in the succeeding page.

Table 1

Tiruchirapalli District, Annual Plan 2003-04

Sector/ sub sector	*No of units to be financed*	*Credit to be provided*
A. AGRICULTURE		
1. Crop loan	—	4585.00
2. Term loans	19,554	1068.37
3. Activities allied to agriculture	26,219	808.50
Sub Total	45,773	6461.87
B. INDUSTRIES		
1. Rural & cottage Industries	6,040	900.77
2. Small Scale Industries	628	848.38
Sub Total	6,668	1749.15
C. SERVICES		
1. Transport Operate	804	607.44
2. Retail Trade & Small Business	25,625	759.00
3. Professional & Self employed	12,075	421.75
Sub Total	38,504	1788.19
D. OTHERS		
1. Education & Loans	257	7.81
2. Housing Finance to Weaker-section	540	26.90
3. Consumer purpose loans	3,035	8.80
Sub Total	3,832	44.59
Grand Total	94,777	10043.80

Source : Primary Data.

This chart is used by the researcher to illustrate scheme wise achievement of loans in the year 1990. December 1999. Prominent sectors like Agriculture, Industries and services sectors have been assigned greater and immense importance in the allocation of loans by the bank.

From the table one can easily assess the target for the various sector fixed by the various sector fixed by the Annual Action Plan and its actual achievement among the sectors during April 1991 to December 1991. Agricultural sector receives the lion's share which includes crop loan, minor irrigation tractors, power pillars and other purposes loans. Besides allied agricultural activities like dairy works, poultry works and other have also been received good attention by the Annual Action Plan in this district. The total financial assistance to agricultural sector was calculated as Rs. 14,387. Similarly the total financial assistance to the physical units as 1,13,163 numbers.

The respective figure for other sectors like Rural artisans, Cottage and SSI and services sectors, targets have also been calculated as Rs. 3,213 and Rs. 16,702 In the same manner the actual achievement for the various sectors have also been presented in the table. Among the schemes wise plan, Government sponsored schemes like I.R.D.P., Self Employment Programme for Urban Poor., have also been received good attention by the Annual Action Plan in this district.

Table 2

Showing the Annual Credit Plan 2003-04 Tiruchirapalli District Sector-wise/Scheme-wise Achievement for the Period April to March 2003-04

Particulars	*Target for the year 1993-92*		*Achievement during April 92 to march 93*		
	Phy. Units	*Fin. Asst.*	*Phy. Units*	*Fin. Asst.*	*Percentage*
I Agriculture					
Crop Loan					
i. Paddy	—	148971	52360	187649	126
ii. Sugarcane	—	90010	6865	39119	43
iii. Banana	—	51038	16163	71276	140
iv. Groundnut	—	35693	3976	21613	61
v. Other Crops	—	197770	68891	282152	142
Total Crop Loans		523482	148255	601809	115
II Term Loans					
a. Minor Irrigation (Incl.pumpsets)	6632	78953	5014	51505	65
b. Tractors /Power Tillers/ Threshers etc.	2482	59129	1932	42764	72
c. Other Purpose	5041	34414	7114	36615	101
Total Loans	14155	172496	14060	130884	76
III Allied Activities					
a. Dairy	12449	54562	9910	40485	74
b. Poultry	2711	18491	599	6807	37
c. Others	8406	40110	10282	51576	128
Total Allied Activities	23566	113163	20791	98868	87
Total	37721	285659	34851	229752	103
IV Rural Artisans & Cott. And SSI	8778	17774	237109	67446	78

V Services	32371	750	285877	—	78
Total Priority Sector Advances	88281	2215	808645	—	93
a. I.R.D.P.	16785	183047	56584	5303	
b. SEEUY	839	224754	18440	21546	
c. SEPUP	1207	637553	3415	637553	

Source : Primary Data.

This table is used to represent item-wise of loans among various sectors disbursed by the Annual Action Plan in this district. The total target for the 1999-90 to the agricultural sector was Rs. 37,722 to the physical units of 809141. Similarly target for other sectors like rural artisans, cottage and SSI and services sector loans disbursement was clearly presented. In the total loans I.R.D.P. received the lion's share i.e., Rs. 15,774 to 67,646 physical units. It was followed by SEEP Programme. In general, most of the programmes had been achieved nearly to its total target.

This table clearly shows the Annual Credit Plan for the year 2001-2000 in Tiruchirapalli District. If it briefly summarized the relationship between the annual target fixed by the researcherity and is the actual achievement made by the bank in this district.

Table 3

Annual Credit Plan 2001-2002. Tiruchirapalli District Sectorwise/Schemewise Achievement for the Period 2003-2004

Particulars	*Target for the Year*		*Achievement during April 94 to March 95*		
	Unit	*Amount*	*Unit*	*Amount*	*%*
I Agriculture					
Crop Loan					
1. Paddy	—	127928	39860	166848	130
2. Sugarcane	—	133008	29534	149399	112
3. Banana	—	91062	4545	39561	43
4. Groundnut	—	59414	13936	66288	112
5. Other Crops	—	194631	54497	322840	166
Total Crop Loans	—	606043	142372	744936	123
II. TERM LOANS:					
a. Minor Irrigation (including Pump sets)	7486	79269	4593	60467	76
b. Tractors/Power Tiller Threshers etc.,	1375	68956	1651	60200	87
c. Other purpose	5343	48560	8857	61033	126
Total Term Loans	14204	196785	15101	181700	92
III. ALLIED ACTIVITIES					
a. Dairy	10385	778119	291227	5933	120
b. Poultry	355	50786	811025	21908	67
c. Others	10493	13869	12065	198961	112
Total Allied Activities	21233	71646	592	60996	111
Total Agriculture	42466	136301	132553	3903	115
IV RURAL ARTISANS & COTTAGE & SSI	7151	272602	25910	80608	99
V. SERVICES TOTAL	28502	247196	171120	150907	85

PRIORITY SECTOR ADVANCES		
	245811	
	247348	
	789573	106

Source : Primary Data.

The above table is used to illustrate the sectorwise and schemewise achievement for the period of April 2001to March 2002. During 1990 up to March 1991 the total target for agricultural sectors loan was calculated as Rs.35437 lakhs. Which includes crop loan, Term loans, Minor irrigation work and allied activities like dairying, poultry, and others. From this table, we could observe that the bank has sanctioned loans to the target level. Other sectors loan distribution is also clearly indicated.

Review of Implementation of Annual Action Plan 1999-2000 during the period from 2001 to 2002

Review of implementation of Annual Credit Plan 1999-90 indicates a collective performance of financial institutions to the extent of 71% which is slightly lesser than proportionate target of 75%. In absolute terms an assistance of 94.01 crores was extended benefiting to Priority Sector and weaker sector categories as against the full years target of 134.21 crores planned.

Sectorwise analysis indicates that the primary Sector Agriculture had bagged the lion's share of assistance to the extent of 64.11 crores to benefit 144684 persons, the quantum of assistance representing 79% of the target for this prime sector under the plan during the review period.

A review of individual schemes reveal that short term credit has been provided to 121888 persons for raising the tune of Rs. 48.49 crores. Medium Term Credit was extended to 8409 persons for Rs. 8.62 crores for schemes like Tractor power tillers/Plough Bullocks/ Carts/Minor Irrigation etc. Credit assistance of Rs. 7.00 crores were extended to 14387 persons for activities like dairy, sheep/goat rearing, biogas development, fishery, sericulture, poultry, duckery, calf rearing etc.

The secondary sector, namely, Industries, had netted a credit flow of Rs. 11.62 crores vis-à-vis the total allocation of Rs. 24.71 crores benefiting 3213 people for activities like handlooms, artisans/Craftsmen's category and other small scale industries units. The percentage of achievement is 49% which is lower than proportionate percentage of 75%.

The tertiary sector, namely services includes the schemes like transport operators, retail trade, small business, professionals and self employed persons. Assistance for education purposes, housing for weaker sections and consumption loans have also been included under this tertiary sector, under these schemes. Financial Institutions have helped 16702 persons with a credit assistance of Rs.18.28 crores while the outlay envisaged for this sector under the plan is Rs.28.58 crores.

Student 't' Distribution

Student 't' distribution is a statistical tool for the small samples (sample size is less than 30) to testify its significance. This is a statistical tool in order to testify the difference between the means of two independent samples. After obtaining the calculated value, we have to compare it to the table value and come to conclusion.

't'	= Test of significance
't'	= x3-x2/s sqrt (n1.n2) / n1+n2)
Where x1	= Average of sample –I
x2	= Average of sample - II
'S'	= Combined Standard Deviation
n1	= Number of small sample – I
n2	= Number of small sample –II

Ho: There exists a significant difference in branch expansion before and after the introduction of Annual Action Plan Scheme.

Table 4

I Before the Introduction of Annual Action Plan

Year	*No. of Branches*
1965	174
1966	178
1967	183
1968	184
1969	194

Table 5

II After the Introduction of Annual Action Plan

Year	*No. of Branches*
1970	206
1971	233
1972	265
1973	303
1974	374

Table 6

x^1	x^2	(x3-x2)	$(x3-x1)^2$	$(x3-x2)^2$	$(x3-x2)^2$
		(-163)			(276)
174	206	+11	121	-70	4900
178	233	+15	225	-43	1849
183	265	+20	400	-11	121
184	303	+21	441	+27	729
194	374	+31	961	+98	9604
913	1381	2148	17203		
x^1	x^2	$(x3-x1)^2$	$(x3-x2)^2$		

Where x^1 = 162.6

Sx2 = 276.2

Σn1 = 5;

Σn2 = 5

$\Sigma(x3-x1)^2$ =2148

$\Sigma\ (x3-x1)^2$ =17203

Student 't' distribution

$$'t' = \Sigma(x^1 - x^2)\ /s \quad X\ (n^1.n^2)\ /\ (n^1+n^2)$$

$$\text{where } S = \frac{\Sigma\ (x^3-x^1)^2 + \Sigma(x^3-x^2)^2}{(n^1 + n^2) - 2}$$

162.6 - 276.2 / S X 5x5 / 5+5 = 25/10 =2.5

=114.6 x

$$S = \frac{(2148) + 17203}{5+5\ -2} \quad 19351/8 \quad = 2418.7 = 49.1$$

$$'t' = 114.6\ /49.1 \quad x1.6 \quad =4.68$$

Calculated value of 't' =4.68

Since the table value of 't' for (5+5-2) 8 deg. Of freedom 7.87 at 5 per cent level.

So the calculated value of 't' = 4.68 which is less than the table value of 't'= 5.87

There exists a significant difference in branch expansion before and after expansion under Annual Action Plan scheme in Tiruchy District.

Disbursement of loans among industry and services sectors differ significantly during 1988-99 to 1999-2000 under Annual Action Plan Scheme in Trichy District.

Year	Industry Rs. In lakhs X1	Services Rs. In lakhs X2	2314 (x3-x1)	(x3-x1)2	(x3-x2)2	(x3-x2)2
1999-2000	2664	2927	+350	122500	+295	87025
2001-2000	1750	1831	-564	318096	-1090	1188100
2000-01	2371	2858	+54	2916	+266	51076
2003-02	2471	2912	+157	24649	280	78400
	9256	10528		468161		1404601
	x^1	x^2		$(x^3-x^1)^2$		$(x^3-x^2)^2$

$x^1 = x^1/n^1 =$ 9256/4 =2314

$x^2 = x^2/n^2 =$ 10528/4 =2632

$(x^3-x^1)2$ =468161

$(x^3-x^2)2$ =1404601

$n^1 = 4;$

$n^2 = 4;$

$x^1 = 2314$

$x^2 = 2632$

Interfere ration:

The calculated value of 't' =0.8767

Since the table value of 't' for (4+4-2) 6 deg. Of freedom at 5 per cent level=4.13

So the calculated value is less than the table value. So we accept the hypotheses.

(i.e) Disbursement of loans among Industry and services differ significantly during 1999-2000 to 2000-02 under the Annual Action Plan Scheme in Tiruchirapalli district is accepted.

$u_0 = u_1$

9

Findings, Suggestions and Conclusion

In the preceding chapters the working of Annual Action Plan in certain areas of Trichirapalli District, has been discussed. A detailed analysis is made on the field of its activities.

Findings

The major findings are given below:

- In the last 3 years 2000-2003 agricultural sector received greater attention under the Annual Action Plan scheme.
- It was observed that the allocation of crop loan, diary loans and self-employment scheme loans have received greater attention.
- Advances to the weaker sections in priority sector made by the bank in this district has been to the small and marginal farmers followed by I.R.D.P. In the case of the implementation of the Annual Action plan during 1998-2000,

The I.O.B. in Tiruchirapalli District has always exceeded the total target.

- Indian Overseas Bank in Trichirapalli District is act as a Annual Action Plan with the total branches of 103 both in rural centers. In the classification of the banking division, the entire district is broadly classified into four division namely:

    1. Ariyalur Division
    2. Musiri Division
    3. Karur Division
    4. Tiruchirapalli Division

- In most of the branches the branch managers are asked to act as Annual Action Plan Officer/ Co-ordinators. There personnel are sole deciding researcherity in distributing loans and they are also responsible for collecting the loan amount.

- There is no uniformity in the distribution of loans to various sector in urban and in rural banks, in the study area. In general the overall deposit position of Indian Overseas Bank in all the branches in this district was calculated separately the rural banks have mobilized Rs. 49.27 crores, Rs. 30.71 crores in semi-urban branches and Rs. 27.38 in the urban branches have been mobilized. Likewise, the advances position has also been calculated in 1993-94. The total amount of overdue under priority sector was calculated as Rs. 14.03 crores. The percentage of overdues to total advances is calculated as Rs. 19.41 crores.

- The performance of Indian Overseas Bank in the implementation of L.B.S may be considered as generally satisfied. While remarkable success has been achieved in certain areas. There is still scope for accomplishment of other objectives. As pointed out earlier in branch expansion it has achieved commendable success.
- Preparation of credit plan is an important function of the Annual Action Plan. Although Indian Overseas Bank has prepared detailed credit plans, it is subjected to criticism for being unrealistic. A review of targets and achievements support this view point. In most of the case the performance is very much lower than the target. In some other cases their performance is very much lower than the target. In an exercise of such a great magnitude total perfection cannot be expected. The disconcerting fact is that there is yawing gap between achievement and target. There is no room for complacence, simply because achievement is more than allocation. This may well be attributed to the unrealistic targets fixed.
- In order to make the district credit plan ore realistic there must be a critical assessment of implementation of earlier credit plans. The administrative, legal and procedurals, bottlenecks have to be identified. It has been found that sufficient attention has not been paid to these areas. The banks which failed to achieve the targets were not even asked for an explanation.
- A more detailed discussion in the D.C.C and S.I.B.C meetings on the progress in respect of

credit disbursement under major schemes and the operational lacunae would provide an opportunity to understand the myriad difficulties. Banks have been encouraging in the task of rural development under the L.B.S.

- The failures of some banks to achieve the credit allocations may be because of the fact each branch of a bank has its own business target fixed by its Head Office. Taking this and their manpower position into account the District Credit Plan have to be streamlined.
- The D.C.P for 1998- states that the number of field/technical staff and officers with the public sector banks is inadequate. Generally each field/ technical officers has to cover 2 or 3 branches and serve a number of loan accounts. Even some of the public sector banks- State Bank of Mysore, Allahabad Bank, Dena Bank, New Bank of India Punjab and Sind Banks and Vijaya Bank do not have field/ technical officers. As regards private sector banks, the services of technical staff/ Agricultural officers are not available at their branches.
- For the implementation of the Credit Plan the banks should have necessary financial resources. The important sources of funds to support the implementation of the D.C.P are deposits mobilized by commercial banks, funds available under different schemes, margin provided by various bodies like DIC & SIDCO, refinance from NABARD/IDBI etc. But the satisfactory performance depends very much on the recovery of loans. On an average the recovery percentage

is estimated to be around only 60%. Apparently the recovery drive must be undertaken seriously. Top priority has to be given to the aspects of timely recovery. So that the bankers morale is kept high and borrowers' attitude towards banks remains one of honestly and integrity.

- For example, the following functions assigned under LDS have been neglected altogether.
- Identifying industrial, commercial and other establishments and farms which do not have banking accounts and increasing their owned resources through the creation of surpluses from additional production financed from the banking system.
- Examining the facilities for marketing of agricultural produce and industrial production storage and undertaking space and the linking of credit with the marketing.
- Surveying the facilities for stocking of fertilizers and other agricultural inputs and the repairing & servicing of equipments.
- The Indian Overseas Bank has been playing a lead role of a liaison agency and it motivates/ induces of coordination for the development of the district But the government agencies and institutions were virtually ancient, to integrate with functions of the various departments, and with the Annual Action Plan. Thus the Indian Overseas Bank tries to remove the crippling organizational gaps. Though, these trails are made, it never gives practical application.
- Agriculture is the primary sector of Trichy

District. It has not been very profitable. The Marketable surplus is not being enlarged. Various agricultural operations are carried out in the traditional manner. Elements of modernization have not been noticed.

- More than 25 crops are cultivated in the district. But paddy is the major crop. Its cultivation covers more than 40% with adequate assured water facilities. The district enjoys a fairly good cropping intensity.
- The productivity in agriculture is relatively low in this district. The pattern of land utilization is not very encouraging. Vast stretches of waste lands are available.
- Large scale, medium scale and small scale industrial units are gradually coming up. Still Trichy District is an industrially backward district. The Annual Action Plan evinces great interest in assisting all types of industrial efforts in order to ensure a comprehensive and balanced development of the industrial sector.
- The Annual Action Plan scheme has been introduced in early seventies in this district. But the year of effective implementation of the Annual Action Plan scheme seems to be 1979. The lead role has been assigned to the Indian Overseas Bank which is having more than 30 branch offices.
- Spatial imbalances are also found as far as branch banking is concerned. Some towns have too many banks and they suffer from multiplicity of credit institutions. At the same time there are many centers in rural area which do not

have any bank at all or which have just a single bank branch. Applying the norms of modern commercial banking there imbalances are not justified in any way. There imbalances should be rectified effectively.

Suggestions

In the light of the above discussion, the researcher has recommended the following suggestions for the betterment and to increase effective functioning of the banking activity in this district. Even though I.O.B. is the Annual Action Plan in this area it is not in a position to care to the entire financial needs of the sectors in this district under J.V.V. (Jawahar velai vaippu thittam) and J.R.Y. (Jawahar Rozhar Yojana) Scheme, T.S. Grama Swarna Jayanthi Yojana Tamil Nadu government have instructed the banks to sanction more volume of loans in the development of rural sector.

1) Most of the schemes implementation by the government always face hardship of financial constraints. The banking researcherities are in a position to sanction only a limited volume to the target groups. So, the government and the banks must increase their loan amount to meet the entire needs of the people.

2) Definitely the Annual Action Plan is an instrument for the implementation of social objectives. There fore several sectors such as agriculture S.S.I., etc. Which despite their importance from the National income point of view did not receive adequate attention from the banking sector.

3) Regarding the service area approach followed by the concerned Annual Action Plan. The bank should taken into account the future development of the particular area.

4) Under the priority sector scheme, the banks were directed to earmark more and more credit for the priority sector and the rural areas. Specifically Tiruchirappalli district is the agricultural belt in Tamil Nadu and so, the target for priority sectors has to be increased.

5) In the identification of a particular person in the priority sector i.e in agriculture, cottage, S.S.I. small farmer, marginal farmer rural artisans, self employed persons and poultry etc .

6) At present 25% of the share of bank credit is distributed to the vulnerable sections of society in the priority sector. So the government should come forward to increase the percentage 40% of credit to the priority sector in Tiruchirappalli district.

7) Most of the Annual Action Plan officers and programme coordinators have to face hardship in the collection of overdues from the creditors.

8) Under the thrust of service area approach most of the banks have not disbursed loans to industry or services sectors in this district.

9) At present District Consultative committee is concerned 4 times in an year.

10) The Annual Action Plan officers in rural branches are very reluctant to sanction loans to industrial sector. This type of tendency has to be changed.

11) District Credit Plan: The Annual Action Plans were asked to highlight the particular programme of lending such as I.R.D.P. to persons belonging to weaker sections such as S.C., S.T. and differential rate of interest beneficiaries etc. It should be widened to other programmes such as TRYSM and J.V.Vs, J.V.V. Thittams also.

12) Target groups: Regarding the target group schemes must be made to bring the economic conditions of small farmers. Marginal farmers, share croppers, rural artisans and craftsmen and SC, STs who live below the poverty line I.O.B. in this district is asked to make a survey about their economic conditions in this district.

13) Banking in India had started in the conservative Scottish tradition. Banks restricted their financial activities to commercial and traditional industries. They had been very chary of financing new enterprises or encouraging new ventures.

14) The level of coordination between commercial banks as well as state government departments do not seem to be satisfactory.

15) There is much scope for improving things so far as the development of banking habit among the rural masses is concerned.

16) In a village bank branch frequent transfers of staff should not be effected. For an officer it takes some fears to study the local conditions and people when he is due to asses some relevant things he finds himself transferred to a different place.

17) At times such importance is given by the credit plan to priority sectors alone.

18) The village adoption programme deserves better treatment.

19) Certain administrative, procedures may be simplified adjusted and relaxed. Rigid rules must be changed suitable substitutes should be introduce.

20) Another important thing is about the necessity to reconstitute the district consultative committee periodically.

Conclusion

In a nutshell, the Annual Action Plan scheme has provided a fruitful framework for the coordinated development of banking at the grass roots level. Its importance has been enhanced in the implementation of the Jawahar Rozhar Yojana and Jawahar Velai Vaippu Thittam and other poverty mitigation programmes in this district. I.O.B. is the pioneering bank in this area and it acts as a leader for the consortium and there is an integrated approach with emphasis on development oriented credit. The district credit plan in Tiruchirappalli district provides the basis for a joint programme of work for financial agencies and district as well as block level functionaries. The expansion of branch banking in the unranked rural areas of the district by starting up of many region rural banks and Annual Action Plan has occupied a provide position. Each and every bank has adopted a particular village and it would be lacking the whole responsibilities by the method of credit plan and area approach to overall development. Under the Annual Action Plan scheme commercial banks have directed to proceed to follow the service area approach in the identified particular centers in Tiruchirappalli district. In a nutshell, the Annual Action Plan is required to act as a catalytic agent for the growth and to provide leadership in initiating and quickening the process of development in this district.

QUESTIONNAIRE/ SCHEDULE : THE ANNUAL ACTION PLAN SCHEME COORDINATORS BANK:

1. Are you satisfied with the method of preparing the DCP? If no, in what ways you are unsatisfied?

2. Do you think that the Credit share allotted to your bank was based on reasonable grounds in 1991, 1992,1993,1994. If no, in what way it is incorrect?

3. In how many times, yours banks had accepted the credit share without 'Bargain' since the first DCP?

4. If it correct, that the allocations made under DCP are to be attained over and above your usual working?

5. Did the DCP, at any time , disturb your working? If yes, in what ways?

6. In your view who should prepare the DCP?

i. Present system is o.k.

ii. A committee comprising of Government officials and Bankers.

iii. Reserve Bank of India.

iv. Government Agencies.

7. Do you believe that DCC is an useful form to

sort out the difficulties and arrive at meaningful conclusion ? If no, please specify how they can be sorted out in the obscene of DCC?

8. Do you find any fault in the constitution of the DCC, If yes, please explain.

9. Are you satisfied with the conduction of DCC meeting? If no, please give reasons.

10. IS it necessary to change the periodicity of DCC meeting? If yes, which would be an ideal periodicity?

11. In your view, how should be the converser of the DCC?

A) A higher Government Officer.

B) A Reserve Bank of India

C) Head Bank officer, as at present.

D) Some other hand other than the head Bank officer,

12. Are you satisfied with the present system of reporting? If no, please specify the difficulty.

13. In your experience, in containing credit to borrowers, had you come across the difficulty of.

a. inadequate

b. lack of infrastructure.

c. Other, please specify

14. It is necessary to have extra-staff to look after the LBS activities?

15. Do your bank, in the district, is inadequately staffed? Yes, clerical........ Technical .... No.

16. What is your percentage of performance to your

Cr. Share in 1991, 1992, 1993, 1994……… ……………Agriculture 1992, 1993, 1994…..Industry 1992, 1993, 1994………… Services 1992, 1993, 1994…………….. could you mention any special reason for the low performance made under DCP? If yes, what is the maximum limit?

17. Do you have the discretionary power to accept the allocations made under DCP? If yes, what is the maximum limit?

Concluding Remarks

It can be observed from the above analysis that the nation has experienced a substantial improvement in both economic and social front along with demographic changes over time. Level of social and economic development are operating simultaneously in bring about a change in the demographic behaviors at the state level. The quantum of net migration is associated mainly with economic development in the sense that states with better economic development have higher rate of immigration and states with lower economic development have higher rate of out migration. The contribution of social development seems to be more pronounced among the states in adopting higher rate family planning methods which in turn is responsible for lowering birth rate. Therefore, the slogan "Development is the best contraceptive" seems to be appropriate in Indian context.

REFERENCES

1. Agrawal, A.N., Varma, H.O. and Gupta, R.C., *India-Economic Information Year Book 1991-92,*

National Publishing House, New Delhi, 1992.

2. Bhattacharjee, Amit K., "Population and Development-Some Policy Issues: in *Population Policy Perspectives in Developing Countries*, Edited Volume by Vatsala Narain and C.P. Prakasam, Himalaya Publishing House, Bombay, 1983.
3. Easterlin, R.A., "Effect of Population Growth on Economic Development of Developing Countries:, *Economic Development and Cultural Change*, Annuals, Vol. 369, 1967.
4. Government of India, "Health Information of India 1992", Central Bureau of Health Intelligence, Ministry of Health and Family Welfare, Nirman Bhavan, New Delhi, 1993.
5. Government of India, "Family Welfare Programme in India, Year Book 1990-91", Department of Family Welfare, Ministry of Health and Family Welfare, New Delhi, 1992.
6. McGranahan, D. V., "Contents and Measurement of Socio-Economic Development, A Staff Study of the U.N. Research Institute for Social Development, New York, 19"Contents and Measurement of Socio-Economic Development, A Staff Study of the U.N. Research Institute for Social Development, New York, 1972.
7. Registrar General, India, "Sample Registration System", Fertility and Mortality indicators, Ministry of Home Affairs, Survey Division., New Delhi, 1992.

United Nation, "The Population Debate: Dimensions and Perspectives", Papers of the World Population Conference, Bucharest, 1972,

Vol, 1, New York, References

8. Bhagwati, J. (2001). Growth, Poverty and Reforms. *Economic and Political Weekly.* March 10.
9. Government of India, (Ministry of Finance), *Economic Survey,* Various Issues.
10. Mishra, S.K.; Puri, V.K. (2001). *Indian Economy.* Himalaya Publishing House, Mumbai-400 004.
11. Nagarajan, R. (1997). What Has Happened since 1991? Assessment of India's Economic reforms; *Economic and Political Weekly.* November 8.
12. Raju, S.S. and Chowdhry, K.R. (1997) New Economic Policy and its impact on Rural Development. In *New Economic Policy and Perspective to Rural Development.* Ed. R.P. Singh. NIRD, Hyderabad.
13. Vyas, V.S. (1996). Agricultural Trade Policy for Nineties: Issues and Approaches. *Economic and Political Weekly,* Vol. 29, No. 26, PP A54-64.
14. Vyas, V.S, (2001). Agriculture: second Round of Economic Reforms. *Economic and Politically Weekly,* March 10.

Bibliography

1. S.S.M. Desai: "Rural banking in India", *Banking in India,* Himalaya Publishing House, Bombay-5, 1979.
2. Ruddar Datt and K.P.M. Sundaram: *Indian Economy,* S. Chand Publications, New Delhi, 1982.
3. R.P. Goyal: *Annual Action Plan Scheme in India,* 1978.
4. Myint, H.: *The Economics of the Developing Countries,* 1965.
5. Rao, V.L.: *Progress of Development Banking Commission,* 1969.
6. Tannan, M.I.: *Banking Loan and Practice in India,* 17th Edition, Bombay 1979.
7. Vasanth Desai : *Indian Banking: Nature and Problems,* Himalaya Publishing House, second edition, 1987.
8. Varde, S.D. Palan Palan S.M.Z.S.: "Branch Banking Organization" Centralisation Vs.

Decentralisation, *Banker's Management*, Bombay-1978.

9. R.P. Goyal: *The Anatomy of Indian Banking*, Himalaya Publishing House, Bombay, 1999.

JOURNALS

1. Basanath Metha : "Annual Action Plan Scheme and preparation credit plans", *Southern Economist*, volume No. 28, July 15, 1999.
2. K. Chandrasekar : "Special Distribution of commercial Banking", *Southern Economist*, volume XXXI , No. 13, September 1986.
3. B.W. Chorley : "Institutional finance for Agricultural Development", *Shubada Asarwatha*, Pune, 1977.
4. I.S. Varshneya: "Bank Nationalization and After", *Yojana*, Volume 30, No. 13, July 16, 1988.
5. Saya Sundaram : "Progress of Indian Banking" First Decades of Nationalization and united commercial Review Volume : XXIV, June 1980.

Index